Managing Faculty Resources

G. Gregory Lozier, *Editor*
The Pennsylvania State University

Michael J. Dooris, *Editor*
The Pennsylvania State University

NEW DIRECTIONS FOR INSTITUTIONAL RESEARCH

PATRICK T. TERENZINI, *Editor-in-Chief*
University of Georgia

MARVIN W. PETERSON, *Associate Editor*
University of Michigan

Number 63, Fall 1989

Paperback sourcebooks in
The Jossey-Bass Higher Education Series

Jossey-Bass Inc., Publishers
San Francisco • Oxford

G. Gregory Lozier, Michael J. Dooris (eds.).
Managing Faculty Resources.
New Directions for Institutional Research, no. 63.
Volume XVI, Number 3.
San Francisco: Jossey-Bass, 1989.

New Directions for Institutional Research
Patrick T. Terenzini, *Editor-in-Chief*
Marvin W. Peterson, *Associate Editor*

New Directions for Institutional Research is published quarterly by
Jossey-Bass Inc., Publishers (publication number USPS 098-830), and
is sponsored by the Association for Institutional Research. The
volume and issue numbers above are included for the convenience of
libraries. Second-class postage paid at San Francisco, California, and
at additional mailing offices. POSTMASTER: Send address changes
to Jossey-Bass Inc., Publishers, 350 Sansome Street, San Francisco,
California 94104. *September 12, 1989*

Editorial correspondence should be sent to the Editor-in-Chief,
Patrick T. Terenzini, Institute of Higher Education, University of
Georgia, Athens, Georgia 30602.

Library of Congress Catalog Card Number LC 85-645339

International Standard Serial Number ISSN 0271-0579

International Standard Book Number ISBN 1-55542-848-7

Cover art by WILLI BAUM

Manufactured in the United States of America. Printed on acid-free paper.

Ordering Information

The paperback sourcebooks listed below are published quarterly and can be ordered either by subscription or single copy.

Subscriptions cost $56.00 per year for institutions, agencies, and libraries. Individuals can subscribe at the special rate of $42.00 per year *if payment is by personal check.* (Note that the full rate of $56.00 applies if payment is by institutional check, even if the subscription is designated for an individual.) Standing orders are accepted.

Single copies are available at $12.95 when payment accompanies order. (California, New Jersey, New York, and Washington, D.C., residents please include appropriate sales tax.) For billed orders, cost per copy is $12.95 plus postage and handling.

Substantial discounts are offered to organizations and individuals wishing to purchase bulk quantities of Jossey-Bass sourcebooks. Please inquire.

Please note that these prices are for the calendar year 1989 and are subject to change without notice. Also, some titles may be out of print and therefore not available for sale.

To ensure correct and prompt delivery, all orders must give either the *name of an individual* or an *official purchase order number.* Please submit your order as follows:

Subscriptions: specify series and year subscription is to begin.
Single Copies: specify sourcebook code (such as, IR1) and first two words of title.

Mail orders to:
Jossey-Bass Inc., Publishers
350 Sansome Street
San Francisco, California 94104

New Directions for Institutional Research Series
Patrick T. Terenzini *Editor-in-Chief*
Marvin W. Peterson, *Associate Editor*

The Association for Institutional Research was created in 1966 to benefit, assist, and advance research leading to improved understanding, planning, and operation of institutions of higher education. Publication policy is set by its Publications Board.

For information about the Association for Institutional Research, write:

AIR Executive Office
314 Stone Building
Florida State University
Tallahassee, FL 32306-3038

(904) 644-4470

Contents

Editors' Notes

This sourcebook should help guide the formulation and implementation of policies about the management of faculty resources at an individual college or university. It is directed equally at institutional researchers and planners and academic administrators.

From literature that has sprouted in recent years (for example, on the status of the professoriate and the faculty labor market, on the dimensions of an academic career, and so on), two important notions have emerged. The first is that faculty are the single most valuable resource of a college or university. The second is that the effective management of that resource is, for a variety of reasons, becoming more and more critical—both for higher education as a whole and for the vitality of individual campuses.

The goal of this volume is to contribute to the effective and efficient management of faculty at individual institutions. By management we do not mean day-to-day direction of individual faculty; rather, we are concerned with the recruitment and development of the professoriate to promote institutional, educational, and societal aims. The authors explore some of the main issues practitioners will want to consider as they raise questions, provide information, and formulate institutional policy to influence the management of faculty resources at the campus level. Each chapter focuses on a single aspect, such as faculty development or affirmative action, and makes pragmatic suggestions for evaluating current practices and developing and implementing new strategies.

The greatest barrier to effective management of faculty resources is the loose or inconsistent application of fundamental policies and procedures for academic personnel. In Chapter One Barbara Lee lays out the essential elements of academic personnel policies and procedures for recruitment, evaluation, promotion and tenure, salary increases, and retirement plans and incentives. This chapter should guide the development and implementation of practices that are ethically, legally, and managerially sound.

Chapter Two explores the area of renewal and change. Shirley Clark and Mary Corcoran investigate the conditions that affect faculty vitality and suggest that most institutions need to take a longer, life-course perspective on faculty careers. The authors suggest a number of strategies for faculty development that may be more productive for both institutions and individuals.

Chapter Three examines the ramifications of nontraditional appointments, which have increasingly been used as alternatives to tenure track positions. David Leslie discusses the conditions that have led to this situation, the benefits and the dangers of nontraditional appointments, and the policy and strategic implications of "creative staffing."

Chapter Four begins with an encapsulation of the history and principles of affirmative action and its effect on academic staffing. Kathryn Moore and Michael Johnson look not only at what campuses must do but just as importantly at what they can do to address affirmative action and equity concerns in areas such as faculty recruitment, evaluation, and support. Attention to these issues encourages the institution to see the advantages of affirmative action initiatives in the development of a quality professoriate.

In Chapter Five Karen Byers, Cynthia Linhart, and Michael Dooris briefly review academic institutions as organizations and re-examine the function of the professoriate to provide a context for discussing the management of faculty. They then look at tools and techniques for allocating faculty resources. For example, they consider issues such as the measurement of faculty workload and the design of workload studies, and they provide overviews of modeling and forecasting techniques.

In Chapter Six Carol Yoannone identifies some of the important information resources on the management of faculty. This annotated bibliography describes a variety of reports, demographic data, studies, and research projects that might be helpful to researchers analyzing the issue from the perspective of an individual college or university.

In the final chapter we examine academic staffing in the context of recent developments in the national market for faculty and suggest that faculty resource management is likely to become both more complex and more critical in the decade ahead.

G. Gregory Lozier
Michael J. Dooris
Editors

G. Gregory Lozier is executive director of planning and analysis at The Pennsylvania State University and a member of the graduate faculty in higher education.

Michael J. Dooris is senior planning analyst in planning and analysis at The Pennsylvania State University.

Sound management of human resources requires policies and procedures that are developed carefully and applied consistently. Monitoring personnel decisions and developing data bases that document their outcomes will help ensure that such decisions not only are made fairly but are perceived to be so by faculty.

Academic Personnel Policies and Practices: Managing the Process

Barbara A. Lee

A recent replication of the famous Caplow and McGee (1958) study of faculty personnel practices concluded that the management of human resources in academic organizations has improved very little in thirty years (Burke, 1987). This study and a study of litigation against colleges by faculty challenging negative employment decisions (LaNoue and Lee, 1987) suggest that the management of the faculty personnel process needs improvement. This chapter will discuss several areas of the employment relationship between the institution and the faculty member. Effective policies and procedures and administrative monitoring of their implementation can improve faculty work life and make the management of the faculty personnel process more effective.

Whether faculty actively participate in academic personnel decisions, it remains the responsibility of administrators—department heads, deans, provosts or academic vice presidents, and ultimately the president—to manage the process appropriately. Once a determination is made of the role of each individual or group in these decisions, it falls to the administration to make sure the process produces decisions that are fair. And because of the ever-present threat of litigation, especially over negative

G. G. Lozier and M. J. Dooris (eds.). *Managing Faculty Resources.*
New Directions for Institutional Research, no. 63. San Francisco: Jossey-Bass, Fall 1989.

tenure decisions, the administration is also responsible for monitoring the process and holding all parties accountable for their actions. (The special role of academic administrators in managing faculty resources is examined further in Chapter Five.)

When the faculty participate in personnel decisions, they too play an important role. At many institutions the faculty are responsible for evaluating a candidate's performance or promise, while administrators assess the fit between the candidate's skills and the institution's needs and determine whether the faculty recommendation is supported by sufficient evidence of performance or promise. At other institutions administrators have sole responsibility for making faculty personnel decisions. Whatever the role of faculty in these important decisions, the administrators' responsibility is to manage the process in the best interests of the institution and to guarantee fairness to the candidates.

As the demographics of our institutions' student bodies shift in the next decade and as the current professoriate ages, creating or worsening shortages of faculty in certain disciplines, the efficient and effective management of the faculty life cycle—from recruitment to retirement and beyond—will become critical. The purpose of this chapter is to provide a benchmark against which faculty and administrators can assess the quality and sufficiency of their faculty personnel policies and procedures. For those institutions whose personnel management systems are well developed, the chapter will suggest strategies for monitoring the process and ensuring its accountability. For other institutions, whose policies and practices still have room for improvement, the chapter will offer approaches that have been effective in other settings.

Recruitment

Once a department has received permission to fill a vacant faculty line or has been given a new line to fill, it then must define the nature of the position. Are there specific curricular and/or teaching needs that must be met or can the department search for the best-qualified candidate in a more broadly defined area and then adjust teaching responsibilities accordingly? In defining the nature of the position, the department is committing institutional resources for a potentially long period (assuming the candidate is awarded tenure several years later), so administrative oversight of the department's decision is critical.

The next step is to establish a search committee that will develop the position description, recruit a pool of candidates, and recommend one or more for selection (Waggaman, 1983). Again, administrative oversight of the committee's composition is important to assure that it represents department-wide interests, understands institutional priorities, and recognizes the importance of affirmative action and other diversity issues.

Appointing a committee member from outside the department, school, or division can help provide a diverse perspective. If at all possible, the committee should include one or more women or minority group members (Ohio State University, 1988).

Academic administrators should be very clear about the search committee's role: Is it to recommend one candidate to the department or a slate of candidates to a department head or dean? What is the deadline for the committee's decision? What will happen if the committee can not identify a suitable candidate or if there is dissension among committee members as to the preferred candidate? To what degree must the committee weigh affirmative action considerations in its decision (Kaplowitz, 1986)? Who decides to reopen a search? Administrators should communicate the answers to these questions before the search process begins, in order to resolve problems quickly and avoid the perception that the administration is biasing the process.

The low representation of racial minorities across disciplines and of women in many disciplines suggests that recruitment of these groups should be much more vigorous than in the past. The success of several institutions in attracting minority faculty is solely attributable, according to institutional representatives, to the priority placed on such recruitment by top administrators and to the resources they provide for it (Heller, 1988). While women are better represented overall among faculty than in earlier years, both women and minority faculty tend to cluster at junior ranks. They are under-represented in scientific and technical disciplines and over-represented in part-time and non–tenure track positions (Aisenberg and Harrington, 1988). Whatever an institution's experience with recruitment from special populations, its efforts will not be successful without strong direction, support, and monitoring by its leadership. At some institutions an offer to hire a faculty member can not be made until the affirmative action office is satisfied that the search committee made a serious attempt to include women and minorities in the pool and that the hiring decision was unbiased. Chapter Four discusses strategies for increasing the presence of under-represented groups on the faculty.

Once the pool has been developed and a "short list" agreed on, most institutions invite candidates for a campus visit. Again, the procedures used for these visits are critical both to the success of the recruitment effort and the fairness of the decision. The institution's expectations for faculty performance, particularly regarding teaching and scholarly productivity, should be made explicit. Either the department chair or the dean (or both) should tell the candidate, both orally and in writing, exactly what to expect during a probationary period (if the hiring is done at a junior rank) so that the individual can determine whether he or she really fits at the institution.

Failure to communicate the institution's standards to the candidate can lead to negative reappointment, promotion, or tenure decisions several years hence. Considering the resources expended in recruiting, hiring, and evaluating junior faculty as well as the personal cost to the candidate and the emotional toll a negative decision may exact from other faculty (Wright, 1985), the failure to make expectations clear or to monitor carefully the progress of junior faculty is simply irrational. If this function is delegated to the department chair, as is the case in many institutions, then it is the responsibility of the administration to make sure this information is conveyed clearly to each candidate, especially when the department's standards may not match the institution's performance standards (Burke, 1987).

Once the campus visits are over, the committee recommends one or a few candidates to the department faculty, the chair, or an academic administrator. The committee may decide that the best-qualified candidate is one whose credentials do not exactly match the job description, while others in the pool fit it more closely. No one need insist that the selected candidate match the job description perfectly; as long as the department can cover its teaching needs and other responsibilities, it should be encouraged to select the candidate who is strongest overall rather than one with a particular subject-matter expertise. Should this strategy be followed, however, the committee must document the reasons for selecting that individual, in the event that a disappointed candidate later sues the institution, arguing that he or she was "better qualified" in terms of the position description. The department head, dean, and academic vice president should be satisfied that such documentation is in place before approving the hiring.

Evaluation

Giving faculty feedback on their performance is critical for several reasons. First is the obvious relationship between constructive feedback and the improvement of performance (Seldin, 1984). But more important for the purposes of this chapter is the close relationship between faculty evaluation and effective decision making in the faculty personnel process. Personnel decisions are expensive and of great significance to the institution's future, particularly at institutions that offer lifetime tenure to faculty.

Most academic administrators probably have some notion of what "acceptable" faculty performance is, although they may differ among themselves and with the faculty. Standards for faculty performance must be articulated if faculty are expected to perform accordingly. While it is unrealistic and probably counterproductive to attempt to define a quantitatively measurable standard for either teaching or scholarly performance, institutions and their academic departments should develop a clear notion of what they expect from faculty. For research universities and other institutions that place a high value on scholarship and publication, each discipline may need to interpret the overall (institutional) performance standard in its own context. For institutions at which faculty are represented by a collective bargaining agent, performance standards may have to be negotiated with the union, although the overall expectations of the institution would generally be a management prerogative (unless state laws specifies otherwise) (Kaplin, 1985).

Untenured Faculty. The communication of performance standards and information on how well an individual is meeting those standards is particularly important during the probationary period. Particularly in institutions where faculty are employed for five or more years before a tenure decision is made, early and frequent feedback on the faculty member's progress toward tenure is critical (Miller, 1987). One strategy used by some institutions is to assign a senior faculty mentor to each junior faculty member to help him or her decide which journals to submit articles to, to assist with teaching if necessary, and to provide advice on winning grants. Probationary faculty should be evaluated annually using the techniques of formative evaluation, which is designed to improve performance (Seldin, 1984, p. 128). There should also be a summative evaluation approximately halfway through the probationary period (when at many institutions a reappointment decision must be made). This "dress rehearsal" for the tenure decision helps the candidate assess his or her progress and prospects for tenure (Hendrickson and Lee, 1983). Departments that wait until the year before the tenure evaluation to assess the candidate's progress do the individual as well as the institution a disservice—it is too late by then.

In academic and nonacademic organizations alike, supervisors are reluctant to evaluate their colleagues and if they do so at all, often inflate their evaluations to avoid hurting candidates or to help them attain better salary increases. Inflation of evaluations, especially for untenured faculty, is worse than not conducting them at all, for it gives the candidate an unrealistic expectation of a positive tenure decision and often leads to litigation. At many institutions untenured faculty members are asked to provide a list of their activities for the previous or current year, including courses taught and developed, research projects, and service to the profession, the institution, or the community. The evaluation should be presented in writing, either before a personal conference with the faculty member or after, as a summary of the oral evaluation.

If department heads conduct the annual evaluation, the administrator at the next level (for purposes of this chapter assume it is the dean) should read the evaluation, assess whether the documentation provided by the faculty member supports the department head's evaluation, and confer with the department head and the faculty member about any difference of opinion. A similar review should be done by the academic vice president at all but the very largest institutions so that performance is evaluated by someone who is familiar with the institution's expectations. Again, discrepancies should be discussed among the administrators and the faculty member. This process may appear time-consuming and cumbersome but, if conducted properly and in good faith, should clearly communicate to the faculty member how his or her performance is viewed. Faculty members who can see that their performance is clearly not meeting the college's expectations may decide to leave rather than endure a negative tenure review. This saves the institution time and money, reduces the sometimes demoralizing impact of a negative outcome on the person's departmental colleagues, and allows the individual to seek a position that better suits his or her interests.

Tenured Faculty. The propriety and even the legality of evaluating faculty once they attain tenure are being vigorously debated. The American Association of University Professors (AAUP) has opposed post-tenure review, stating that it "would threaten academic freedom" (American Association of University Professors, 1983, p. 14a). The Association maintained that the award of tenure insulates a faculty member from periodic review, unless that review is for the purpose of promotion, salary increase, or other benefits, and it strongly opposed using such evaluations as grounds for dismissal or other disciplinary action. Some legal scholars disagree with this position, and it appears quite likely that a system of post-tenure review that was developed carefully and administered fairly would be upheld against legal challenge (Olswang and Fantel, 1980–81).

How the policies and procedures for post-tenure review are developed depends on the reason for doing it. The institution should determine whether the review is for faculty development or for providing evidence for personnel decisions, such as salary increases or other rewards (Seldin, 1984; Andrews, 1985; see also the discussion in Chapter Two on post-tenure faculty renewal and change). To make the review effective, senior faculty should be closely involved in designing the review process and in conducting the review (Licata, 1986). At unionized institutions the decision to review tenured faculty on a periodic basis is generally a management prerogative, although the process for conducting the review and the use to which the information is put must be negotiated with the union.

Academic administrators should monitor the evaluation process to make sure that it is done, that it is conducted fairly, and that it is followed up for both those faculty identified as high achievers and those found to be poor performers. It will likely be difficult to balance the administration's concern for maintaining a high level of faculty performance against the faculty's fear that evaluation results will be used to discharge tenured faculty members inappropriately. Involving faculty in the design and implementation of the review process will help to allay those fears but probably will not extinguish them.

Promotion and Tenure

The decision whether to grant tenure to a faculty member is probably the most important one an institution makes. Giving tenure to marginal candidates housed in a small department can for decades stymie institutional attempts to improve the quality of that department. For that reason careful attention to the policies and procedures used to make the tenure decision, conscientious monitoring of the decision-making process, and some common-sense practices in implementing policies should result in wiser, fairer decisions.

Candidate's Role. It is difficult to generalize about the tenure decision process because of the diversity of institutions and their practices. However, it is usually appropriate for the candidate to have a role in preparing his or her dossier for evaluation by reviewers and in suggesting some of the external reviewers (if they are used). Analysis of court challenges to tenure denials demonstrates that the more open the procedure and the greater the role played by the candidate in the process, the more likely the institutions are to prevail (Lee, 1985).

Peer Review Process. After the candidate's dossier is prepared and the letters from external reviewers are in hand, the institution's review process begins. At most four-year institutions faculty play a major role, at least at the departmental level and often at the college or divisional level as well. Whether or not the faculty are unionized, careful adherence to institutional procedures is critical, particularly during the faculty's review of the candidate, for many institutions regard the peer evaluation as the most important assessment of the faculty member's performance, especially in the areas of scholarship and service. Procedural violations can usually be grieved at a unionized college or university, and may also form the basis for a court challenge. Many judges refuse to overturn peer judgments of performance but have routinely overturned tenure or promotion decisions when substantial procedural violations were found (Lee, 1985; LaNoue and Lee, 1987). This is not to say that the substantive evaluation of a faculty member's performance is not important, but that establishing fair and appropriate tenure and promotion policies and monitoring the compliance of faculty and administrators with those policies and procedures should also make the decisions fairer, both in appearance and in fact.

Thus, when the department, either by committee or as a whole, develops its recommendation, whether positive or negative, that recommendation must be documented carefully and thoroughly. The department should give copies of the guidelines to the faculty member at the time of hiring and subsequently provide copies of annual evaluations. The decision should be made according to this information. Did the candidate live up to the expectations that were communicated to him or her initially and annually thereafter? If so, how was this accomplished? If not, in what specific ways did the candidate fall short? Irrespective of the decision, the department must demonstrate how it has reached its conclusions. How is the candidate's teaching good—or unacceptable—and what data did the decision makers use?

While most judges accept student evaluations of teaching as reasonable evidence of teaching quality, multiple information sources are a better gauge of teaching performance (Centra, 1979; Seldin, 1984; Andrews, 1985). Particularly when teaching is the major criterion for evaluating faculty (the common practice at most community colleges and some four-year institutions as well), review of syllabi and exams, peer observation and feedback, and other evaluation of teaching provide important information and reduce a department's reliance on student opinion.

Similarly, although a candidate's peers are generally regarded as qualified judges of scholarship, publications, and service to the discipline or profession, the addition of evaluations from external experts in the candidate's field provides additional data, which is normally viewed as improving the validity of the decision. The department's decision should refer to all the information used; multiple information sources on a candidate's performance make it difficult for the department to either inflate the quality of that performance or reach a discriminatorily negative decision.

Department Chair's Role. Whether the department chair is considered a part of the administration (as many are on unionized campuses) or a faculty peer, it should be the chair's responsibility to monitor the decision-making process, to make sure the information being relied on is accurate and complete, and to insist that the recommendation be documented carefully. If the chair must make a separate recommendation, this is an opportunity to discuss the department's concerns about the candidate (if any), to describe how the candidate's continued employment will strengthen the department's teaching or research capacity, or to explain splits in the department's vote.

Evaluating the Reviewers. Depending on institutional practice, the next level of review may be either a dean, an institutional-level administrator, or a faculty committee. If the department's review has been in compliance with procedures and its recommendation is thoroughly documented and supported by the evidence, then subsequent levels of review can address the degree to which the department supported the decision rather than evaluate the candidate's performance or promise for future performance.

Should a reviewing committee or individual find discrepancies between the department's recommendation and the candidate's record (whether the recommendation is unduly positive or unfairly negative), two choices can be considered: either the recommendation may be returned to the department for further documentation or explanation, or the next level of review may reverse the department's recommendation. While either approach is legally permissible (unless institutional policies or a union contract specify a particular requirement), external authorities such as arbitrators, civil rights agency personnel, or judges tend to view a remand to the department more favorably than a unilateral reversal by a reviewing administrator or committee (Lee, 1985). This is not to say that the institution must accept the recommendation of a department or faculty group; rather, it is a suggestion that the department be given a second chance to justify its recommendation. If the justification is unsatisfactory, it need not be followed. However, the process will be viewed as procedurally more fair and as more supportive of peer review.

Feedback to the Candidate. What information is given to the candidate during the long and sometimes tortuous decision-making process? At many institutions the candidate is told little or nothing from the time the department begins its deliberations until the board of trustees makes the final decision. While a system that keeps all information secret until the final outcome is decided has been viewed as permissible by courts (*Smith* v. *University of North Carolina,* 1980), it is not a very humane way to deal with personnel decisions. A few institutions have developed systems in which the candidate is informed in writing at every step of the process; some permit the candidate to submit additional information to an individual or body that has made a negative recommendation. This open process is probably most effective at small institutions, where only a few promotion or tenure decisions are made each year, although it should be equally effective at a large institution where faculty personnel decisions are decentralized to the college or divisional level.

Appealing the Decision. At many institutions, whether the faculty are represented by a union or not, they are permitted to appeal negative employment decisions, although some systems do not permit appeals until the board of trustees makes the final determination. In most cases faculty are permitted to assert only procedural challenges to the decision; thus, procedural compliance becomes an important legal concern on unionized campuses. Scholars have found that a grievance process formalizes and rationalizes personnel decisions (Begin, 1978) and probably enhances accountability in the decision process as well (Estey, 1986). However, a grievance system that permits only procedural challenges will focus exclusively on minute procedural niceties rather than the real issue—namely, did the candidate deserve promotion, tenure, and so on? Thus, while grievance systems probably encourage procedural compliance, they do not necessarily address the degree to which a personnel decision is supported by credible evidence (Lee, 1989).

Salaries

While promotion and tenure decisions occur infrequently for a particular faculty member, salary decisions on many campuses are made annually and may be a source of greater friction than the more important decisions addressed above. Some institutions, particularly two-year colleges and colleges where faculty are unionized, have salary schedules that permit little or no flexibility in granting salary increases. The debate over salary practices hinges on the potential unfairness of a system that focuses entirely on merit (because it may permit favoritism, discrimination, or other inappropriate reasons for raises) versus a rigid salary schedule that rewards underachievers equally with high achievers (Pratt, 1988; Marth, 1988; Chait, 1988). However, if an institution has determined that it will use a merit-based salary system, how can procedures be developed to promote fairness and to reward deserving faculty?

While some argue that merit pay enhances an institution's ability to recruit and retain high-quality faculty and to encourage continued high performance (Hansen, 1988), it is legally a more risky situation to make salary decisions that distinguish between individuals than to give them across-the-board percentage increases. The primary legal pitfall is the accusation that salary decisions are discriminatory. Since nearly every faculty member is a member of at least one protected class under civil rights law (that is, individuals over age forty, handicapped individuals, women, ethnic and religious minorities), many salary decisions are subject to legal challenge. Furthermore, salary decisions that are *perceived* as unfair (whether they are or not) reduce the morale and productivity of faculty who receive small increases.

Carefully conducted and well-documented periodic reviews of faculty performance will help avoid legal challenges to merit-pay decisions and should rebut accusations of favoritism or bias. As with performance reviews for other purposes, criteria should be established first. A system that allows faculty to participate in the setting of criteria will normally be viewed by the faculty as fairer. Although the criteria for merit-pay increases should at least include institutional priorities, departments may wish to add others, such as the development of new courses, leadership on important committees, or the procurement of a significant grant or contract. Once these criteria are established, it should be more difficult for a decision maker (a department chair, a dean, or whoever makes the salary recommendation) to inject personal bias into the decision. Although disputes may remain over the weighing of certain criteria (is the publication of a book more important than leadership on the curriculum revision committee?), at least the results will be based on a set of clearly articulated criteria and therefore less subject to the charge of being arbitrary.

Individuals or groups making salary decisions should be held to the same documentation and accountability standards as those responsible for other personnel decisions. On some campuses merit-pay decisions are grievable, which makes the creation of a defensible record important. Even where such decisions are not grievable, decision makers should be subject to accountability requirements in an effort to discourage inappropriate decisions and to enhance the faculty's perception that the system is fair (even though a member may disagree with a particular decision).

Retirement Plans and Options

No issue in faculty personnel has attracted as much attention in recent years as retirement. In 1986 Congress lifted the age-seventy cap from the Age Discrimination in Employment Act of 1967, although it exempted tenured faculty until the end of 1993. Colleges and universities are scrambling to develop early-retirement plans that will provide incentives for tenured faculty whose productivity has declined to leave the institution. However, changes in the tax laws have limited the kinds of financial inducements that institutions can offer, which makes designing such plans very difficult (Teachers' Insurance and Annuity Association/College Retirement Equities Fund, 1988). Furthermore, there is concern that early-retirement plans will entice the most productive faculty to leave, because they can find positions at other institutions, while those who have few alternative employment options will stay at the institution.

To complicate matters, many colleges and universities face shortages of faculty in certain disciplines over the next ten years. A study of thirty-two research universities concluded that serious shortages of arts and science faculty can be expected in the 1990s, while faculty in business disciplines, computer science, allied health, and law tend to be substantially younger and therefore will likely stay at the institution longer (Lozier and Dooris, 1987, p. 5). All of this uncertainty, both legal and demographic, further complicates the difficult issue of faculty retirement.

Despite the concern about the elimination of mandatory retirement, one study concluded that few institutions were in a position to make informed decisions because most had little or no data on retirement patterns or the cost of various retirement programs (Mooney, 1988). Few have examined the age profile of their faculty to determine where shortages may be likely during the coming decade. Certainly the collection and analysis of data by each institution must precede decisions about the design of early-retirement incentives and the faculty to be targeted.

Furthermore, institutions should know what motivates faculty to take advantage of early-retirement programs. Kellams and Chronister (1987) found that the type and number of benefits offered was the most important motivating factor. Financial security and other (nonfinancial) benefits, such as reserved parking, a library card, and an office on campus, encouraged faculty to take advantage of these programs. Other motivators, although only about half as likely to stimulate early retirement, included professional problems (low productivity or burnout), organizational problems (a nonsupportive department or dean, institutional needs to reduce spending), and attractive alternatives for the faculty member to pursue. The authors note that productive faculty appear just as likely to take advantage of early-retirement incentives as unproductive faculty but do so for different reasons. In the study, productive faculty tended to leave for personal reasons such as health rather than because of dissatisfaction with their academic environment or their own performance.

In a review of the research on the effect of early-retirement programs, Chronister and Kepple (1987, p. 55) concluded that while most programs were moderately successful, some were not in that either very few faculty took advantage of them or the most productive scholars left in disproportionate numbers. The 1978 and 1986 amendments to the Age Discrimination in Employment Act dictate that all retirement plans that apply to faculty less than seventy years old (with no age cap as of 1994) be completely voluntary; institutions cannot force faculty to elect early retirement or threaten them with discharge or negative employment conditions if they choose to remain at the college. This leaves designers of retirement incentives in a quandary: how can they entice faculty who are low producers to leave but make working conditions more attractive for high producers? The law does permit institutions to designate certain academic units for reduction in force, and early retirement may be offered to faculty who would otherwise be laid off without having to offer similar incentives to faculty in units where no layoffs are planned. At institutions where programs were developed for such situations, individuals have reported success in reducing the size of their faculty work force at a substantial financial savings to the institution (Kreinin, 1982).

The early experiences of institutions that have designed early-retirement incentives are moderately positive, but many of these programs were designed before the tax-law changes and with an eventual age of mandatory retirement. Assuming that this cap is removed for faculty in 1994, what are the implications for developing policies and procedures to address both changes in tax laws and changes in retirement legislation?

The issue of selective retention of high-performing faculty is equally important, for during the 1990s certain disciplines will face shortages of faculty even greater than those that currently trouble them (Lozier and Dooris, 1987). Therefore, a comprehensive system of faculty personnel management must include information on which faculty the institution would like to continue employing, either because of their high performance levels or because they are in a field where shortages are anticipated, and which faculty it may wish to induce to retire. The role of the office of institutional research is critical in developing a data bank on faculty age, regional and national trends in the supply of faculty by discipline, and institutional plans to add or drop certain academic programs.

After the institution has this information, it may wish to conduct an anonymous survey of its faculty who are over a particular age—perhaps age fifty—to see what they would desire in an early-retirement plan and what, on the other hand, might induce them to stay even if they were eligible to retire. The institution may wish to involve faculty in designing the plan or have a faculty advisory committee react to various options before one or more is put into place. A tax law expert should review the plan in light of the tax implications for both the institution and the enrolling faculty. Even the best-designed incentives will not induce faculty to retire if severe tax consequences ensue.

Assuming that an institution wishes to keep its most productive faculty but divest itself of its less productive faculty, an alternative to designing early-retirement incentives would be using the dismissal-for-cause mechanism when the institution has sufficient evidence of poor performance to do so. It is unlikely that many, if any, institutions would select this option. Not only are formal hearings required for the dismissal of tenured faculty but a lawsuit based on the age discrimination laws is highly probable, especially if the institution attempts to dismiss only those tenured faculty who are over a certain age. In a few instances the performance of a tenured faculty member may be so unprofessional and intolerable that the institution will dismiss that member for cause, but a wholesale use of this strategy as a substitute for mandatory retirement would cause enormous morale problems, would be exceptionally costly, and would probably be ruled a violation of the civil rights laws.

Conclusion

In many academic institutions, personnel decisions are highly decentralized and recommendations by faculty and middle managers (department chairs and deans) often carry substantial weight. This decentralization means that a well-developed and complete data base that tracks personnel decisions on every faculty member is essential to a well-managed college or university. For both planning and accountability reasons, both line and staff managers should know when decisions are made, what the decision or recommendation is at each level, where in the process a particular decision is at any given time, how long the process takes, where bottlenecks or snags develop, and how protected classes fare compared with nonminorities so that institutional leaders can head off problems before they become serious. Data on recruitment pools, promotion and tenure rates of women and minorities, and salary increases are of special importance to ensuring that decisions are both fair and appropriate. Particularly when some faculty perceive inconsistent treatment between different departments, schools, or regional campuses, a comprehensive data base will help the academic community monitor its own behavior, confirm those practices that are appropriate, and correct its errors.

Developing and implementing effective and legal academic personnel policies require the participation of both faculty and administrators, but the management of the process is the clear responsibility of the administration. Good policies are an important component of good academic personnel decisions, yet even a good policy can be used inappropriately in both intended and unintended ways. Therefore, careful monitoring and an insistence that each individual in the decision-making process be fully accountable should lead to fairer, more consistent decisions and should help insure the institution the quality of faculty it needs to carry out its mission.

References

American Association of University Professors. "On Periodic Evaluation of Tenured Faculty." *Academe,* 1983, *69* (6), 1a–14a.

Andrews, H. A. *Evaluating for Excellence.* Stillwater, Okla.: New Forums Press, 1985.

Begin, J. P. "Grievance Mechanisms and Faculty Collegiality: The Rutgers Case." *Industrial and Labor Relations Review,* 1978, *31,* 295–309.

Burke, D. L. "The Academic Marketplace in the 1980s: Appointment and Termination of Assistant Professors." *Review of Higher Education,* 1987, *10,* 199–214.

Caplow, T., and McGee, R. *The Academic Marketplace.* New York: Basic Books, 1958.

Centra, J. A. *Determining Faculty Effectiveness: Assessing Teaching, Research, and Service for Personnel Decisions and Improvement.* San Francisco: Jossey-Bass, 1979.

Chait, R. "Providing Group Rewards for Group Performance." *Academe,* 1988, *74* (6), 23–24.

Chronister, J. L., and Kepple, T. R., Jr. *Incentive Early Retirement Programs for Faculty.* ASHE-ERIC Higher Education Report, no. 1. Washington, D.C.: Association for the Study of Higher Education, 1987.

Estey, M. "Faculty Grievance Procedures Outside Collective Bargaining: The Experience at AAU Campuses." *Academe,* 1986, *72* (3), 6–15.

Hansen, W. L. "Merit Pay in Structured and Unstructured Salary Systems." *Academe,* 1988, *74* (6), 10–13.

Harrington, M., and Aisenberg, N. *Women of Academe: Outsiders in the Sacred Grove.* Amherst: University of Massachusetts Press, 1988.

Heller, S. "Some Colleges Find Aggressive Affirmative-Action Efforts Are Starting to Pay Off, Despite Scarcity of Candidates." *Chronicle of Higher Education,* February 10, 1988, pp. A-12, A-16–A-17.

Hendrickson, R. M., and Lee, B. A. *Academic Employment and Retrenchment: Judicial Review and Administrative Action.* ASHE-ERIC Higher Education Research Report no. 8. Washington, D.C.: Association for the Study of Higher Education, 1983.

Kaplin, W. A. *The Law of Higher Education: A Comprehensive Guide to Legal Implications of Administrative Decision Making.* (2nd ed.) San Francisco: Jossey-Bass, 1985.

Kaplowitz, R. A. *Selecting College and University Personnel: The Quest and the Questions.* ASHE-ERIC Higher Education Report no. 8. Washington, D.C.: Association for the Study of Higher Education, 1986.

Kellams, S. E., and Chronister, J. L. "Life After Early Retirement: Faculty Activities and Perceptions." Paper presented at the Association for the Study of Higher Education Conference, Baltimore, November 22, 1987.

Kreinin, M. E. "Preserving Tenure Commitments in Hard Times." *Academe,* 1982, *68* (2), 37–45.

LaNoue, G. R., and Lee, B. A. *Academics in Court: The Consequences of Faculty Discrimination Litigation.* Ann Arbor: University of Michigan Press, 1987.

Lee, B. A. "Balancing Confidentiality and Disclosure in Faculty Peer Review: Impact of Title VII Litigation." *Journal of College and University Law,* 1982–83, *9,* 279–314.

Lee, B. A. "Federal Court Involvement in Academic Personnel Decisions: Impact on Peer Review." *Journal of Higher Education,* 1985, *56,* 38–54.

Lee, B. A. "Grievance Systems: Boon or Bane for Shared Governance?" In J. H. Schuster and L. H. Miller (eds.), *Governing Tomorrow's Campus.* New York: ACE-Macmillan, 1989.

Lee, B. A., and Olswang, S. G. "Legal Parameters of the Faculty Employment Relationship." In J. C. Smart (ed.), *Higher Education: Handbook of Theory and Research.* Vol. 1. New York: Agathon, 1985.

Licata, C. M. *Post-Tenure Faculty Evaluation: Threat or Opportunity?* ASHE-ERIC Higher Education Report no. 1. Washington, D.C.: Association for the Study of Higher Education, 1986.

Lozier, G. G., and Dooris, M. J. "Is Higher Education Confronting Faculty Shortages?" Paper presented at the Association for the Study of Higher Education Conference, Baltimore, November 22, 1987.

Marth, E. C. "Merit Pay: Elm Street or Hollywood Boulevard?" *Academe,* 1988, *74* (6), 17–18.

Miller, R. I. *Evaluating Faculty for Promotion and Tenure.* San Francisco: Jossey-Bass, 1987.

Mooney, C. J. "College Officials Are Worrying About an Aging Faculty, But Few Have Plans to Deal with Issues, Study Finds." *Chronicle of Higher Education,* January 6, 1988, pp. A-11, A-13.

Ohio State University. *Handbook for Faculty Searches.* Columbus: Ohio State University, 1988.

Olswang, S. G., and Fantel, J. I. "Tenure and Periodic Performance Review: Compatible Legal and Administrative Principles." *Journal of College and University Law,* 1980–81, *7,* 1–30.

Olswang, S. G., and Lee, B. A. *Faculty Freedoms and Institutional Accountability: Interactions and Conflicts.* ASHE-ERIC Higher Education Report no. 5. Washington, D.C.: Association for the Study of Higher Education, 1984.

Pratt, L. R. "Merit Pay: Reaganomics for the Faculty?" *Academe,* 1988, *74* (6), 14–16.

Seldin, P. *Changing Practices in Faculty Evaluation: A Critical Assessment and Recommendations for Improvement.* San Francisco: Jossey-Bass, 1984.

Smith v. *University of North Carolina*, 632 F.2d 316 (4th Cir. 1980).

Teachers' Insurance and Annuity Association/College Retirement Equities Fund. *Voluntary Incentive Early Retirement Programs.* Research Dialogues no. 18. New York: Teachers' Insurance and Annuity Association/College Retirement Equities Fund, July 1988.

Waggaman, J. S. *Faculty Recruitment, Retention, and Fair Employment: Obligations and Opportunities.* ASHE-ERIC Higher Education Report no. 2. Washington, D.C.: Association for the Study of Higher Education, 1983.

Wright, T. H. "Faculty and the Law Explosion: Assessing the Impact—A Twenty-Five Year Perspective (1960–85) for College and University Lawyers." *Journal of College and University Law,* 1985, *12,* 363–379.

Barbara A. Lee is an associate professor in the Department of Industrial Relations and Human Resources at Rutgers University, where she directs the graduate program. She was a member of the National Institute of Education Study Group on the Conditions of Excellence in Higher Education, a coauthor of the study group's report, Involvement in Learning, *and coauthor (with George LaNoue) of* Academics in Court.

The agenda for a vital professoriate in an era of great changes in higher education requires of administrators a long-term perspective on faculty careers, that is, from graduate school through retirement. Faculty renewal can be positively affected through the actions and decisions of individuals and institutional officers.

Faculty Renewal and Change

Shirley M. Clark, Mary E. Corcoran

This chapter is designed to aid administrators toward the better management of faculty resources through attention to the needs and strategies of renewal and change. We direct the discussion toward three ends. First, we encourage a full understanding of the conditions that affect faculty. vitality; second, we argue for taking a longer, life-course perspective on faculty careers; and third, we advocate consideration of strategies for improving career development.

This discussion is written in the context of the late 1980s. It is a confusing context, for many of the predictions of national councils and study groups of the 1970s have not fully materialized. For example, enrollment in the 1980s has been greater than predictions suggested. Faculty hiring has continued, albeit at an uneven pace. In fact, anticipated retirements among faculty in the next decade may result in shortages at a time when there are only small cohorts of graduate students available to replenish them (El-Khawas, 1988). As expected, the financial outlook for higher education is less favorable than at any time since 1955, and "the conditions and expectations of faculties are correspondingly bleak" (Bowen and Schuster, 1986, p. 7). Tempering this conclusion somewhat is the finding from a recent national survey of over four thousand faculty in 140 small liberal arts colleges that morale and satisfaction have not deteriorated as much as expected (Rice and Austin, 1988).

Academic personnel policies and practices that were shaped largely in

G. G. Lozier and M. J. Dooris (eds.). *Managing Faculty Resources.*
New Directions for Institutional Research, no. 63. San Francisco: Jossey-Bass, Fall 1989.

the post-World War II expansion come increasingly into question with today's circumstances. These circumstances include: longer faculty careers (to become potentially even longer when mandatory tenured-faculty retirement is eliminated in 1994), more-restricted mobility between institutions, limited opportunities for new hiring, and increased expectations for the effectiveness of faculty in student outcomes and in research productivity. These conditions, as well as opportunities and challenges that are likely to arise in the future, need to be kept in mind as institutions plan for the 1990s.

Discussion of faculty resources should not be limited to existing faculty, although there is some tendency to do so during a period of limited growth. Now that prospects of shortages are indeed emerging, a sometimes overlooked aspect of faculty vitality comes into focus, namely, the degree to which faculty careers are perceived as attractive and the extent to which faculty themselves attract and encourage others to such careers. This of course relates to issues of quality as well as quantity and points to a potential area for institutional research.

Faculty careers have a great deal in common with the careers of professionals who work in other organizations. However, because faculty careers have some unique characteristics (for example, tenure), the management of such careers is rather different from the management of personnel in other settings. Therefore, we need to keep in mind the nature of faculty careers and the changing circumstances of higher education as we think about issues of faculty vitality, renewal, and change. We turn now to an exploration of faculty development from an institutional perspective.

Faculty Professional Development

In the United States faculty quality and vitality have long been concerns of institutions. For example, sabbatical leaves for scholarship and refreshment have been available at many colleges and universities since Harvard University introduced the practice in 1810. But when we think of faculty development programs, we most likely have in mind deliberate and systematic policies and provisions dating only to the 1960s and 1970s. By 1976 more than seven hundred colleges and universities reported that they provided some form of faculty development program (Centra, 1978). Since then, as recently demonstrated in an extensive literature search by Bland and Schmitz (1988), at least four hundred articles and books have been published on the subject. But many of these programs may be considered of relatively low priority and permanency by the rate at which they have fallen to the budget ax under the straitened financial conditions of the 1980s.

As a campus personnel "movement," recent faculty development programs have been driven largely by the objective of improving instruction and revising courses and curricula. Major higher education associations and philanthropic foundations such as Lilly, Danforth, and Kellogg generously supported these endeavors. More recently, probably as evidence of the movement's maturation and as a response to basic survival needs facing many institutions, a few faculty development programs have addressed individual and organizational development issues. These include personal growth, career counseling, training or retraining opportunities, and organizational components such as working environment and climate. However, for the most part, individual faculty renewal rather than institutional renewal has been and continues to be the primary emphasis.

Institutional Perspective. We have come to understand that faculty and institutional vitality are interrelated concepts (Clark, Corcoran, and Lewis, 1986). Career vitality is affected at least as much by professional socialization and by organizational structure and conditions such as mission and rewards as it is by personal variables such as intelligence and personality. The ideal faculty types and the emphasized criteria for faculty performance will differ according to institutional type and mission. Institutions that emphasize teaching or service will need to focus more on revitalizing routine teaching and retraining faculty for new curricular emphases. Liberal arts colleges, community colleges, and comprehensive institutions, for example, may broadly define scholarship as keeping current in the discipline and incorporating new knowledge into teaching on a regular basis. While some faculty at these college do pursue research leading to publication, it is expected that their scholarship will be embedded in a primary commitment to integrate new knowledge into good teaching, as implied in the mission of the institution.

Research-oriented universities, somewhat in contrast, will define vital faculty as those who engage wholeheartedly in state-of-the-art research in their fields in addition to satisfying other expectations, such as good teaching. Criteria for advancement in rank, tenure, and salary adjustment will exemplify this orientation. Faculty development programs will need to reflect the importance of research and scholarship in the mission of the institution. In sum, the situation and context of careers in organizations must be given special attention in the customization of faculty renewal policies and programs.

Shared Responsibility. Whose responsibility is faculty vitality? Our response is that both the faculty member and the institution (colleagues, administrators, organizational policies, programs, and structures) share the responsibility for assuring career growth and faculty development. In the past, both faculty and administrators behaved in accordance with the ethic that the success or failure of faculty members was attributable to personal characteristics. Certainly faculty members are socialized as graduate students to value the norms of freedom and autonomy and to solve their productivity problems without much help from peers, the department chair or dean, or faculty development programs. They are educated to be problem solvers, and this expectation is internalized.

In our research on faculty vitality, we found that faculty members in a research-oriented university see themselves as primarily responsible for their careers; in particular, the sample of faculty considered by their peers to be highly active tended to take an assertive, resourceful approach to career problems and blockages (Corcoran and Clark, 1985). Nevertheless, faculty do think that colleagues could be helpful to one another when facing careers that are "stuck" rather than "moving." Very few reported receiving any specific help from institutional sources such as department chairs or deans. In the last section of this chapter, we will have more to say about fixing responsibility for faculty development.

Life-Course Perspective on the Faculty Career

The vitality of individuals, including academics, is often viewed as a life-course phenomenon in a disturbingly linear way in Western societies. Beliefs about the relationship between aging and productivity commonly hold that the die is cast early and immutably with respect to the establishment of personality, identity, work orientations and preferences, and output levels. The assumption of a negative correlation between aging and work performance is explicit in the literature on the graying professoriate and in the support for exempting tenured faculty from the elimination of mandatory retirement age under the 1986 Amendments to the Age Discrimination in Employment Act.

Theories of aging and work abound; most can be classified as biological-physiological, psychological, economic, or sociological. Since there is neither space nor justification to describe each of these approaches here, let us simply point out that faculty developers draw extensively from psychological and sociological theories of development and aging for their strategies and programs. The life-course perspective combines elements from psychological and sociological approaches. It recognizes the personal experience of the career over the life span, the interaction between the individual and his or her social environment over the life course, and the changes in the broader environment that affect the life-course patterns of individuals or cohorts (Blackburn and Lawrence, 1986). In so doing, it avoids positing deterministic (ontogenetic) career-stage models and overemphasizing social structures and norms to the neglect of individual attributes (for example, personality) that can affect performance.

Recently some scholars of the professoriate have attempted to combine classic theories of career development with adult occupational socialization to illuminate what happens to faculty over time and to suggest opportunity for intervention. In this frame of reference, a career moves on a patterned path within an organization (Glaser, 1968). Metaphors of streams and escalators can be used to depict the movement of personnel through an organization (Becker and Strauss, 1956). While an adult may see organizational careers as a series of separate experiences and adventures through which an individual passes, the organization may view careers with a set of expectations that guide its decisions about whom to move, when and how to move them, and how quickly (Shein, 1968). Thus careers might be conceptualized as a series of choices, expectations, identities, and behaviors by the individual; as recruitment, movement, and time-tracking of personnel by the organization; and as allocation to the various occupational statuses from the perspective of the larger society.

Career Socialization of Faculty Members. The initial or preinitial phase of occupational socialization is usually termed anticipatory socialization. At this early time the individual is forming expectations; transmitting, receiving, and evaluating information; and making decisions about an occupation. One takes on the values of the group to which one aspires.

To draw in new members, however, an occupation must have resources: attractors or comparative benefits and facilitators that help people move into the work (Lortie, 1975). In *American Professors: A National Resource Imperiled* (1986), Bowen and Schuster review the declining compensation and deteriorating work environment of the professoriate that may be associated with a discernible reduction in the flow of exceptional talent to academe. Data from a variety of sources suggest that the career choices of college teaching and scientific research have declined in popularity, and nonacademic professional careers have become more attractive to high-achieving college seniors, American Rhodes scholars, and Phi Beta Kappas (Bowen and Schuster, 1986, pp. 201–230). Attention to faculty compensation and work environment may be necessary to improve the prospect of drawing sufficient numbers of high-quality recruits into graduate school and from there into the professoriate.

Occupational Entry. For most faculty members, anticipatory socialization and early induction to the faculty role occurs during graduate school. This process is quite complex and variable from discipline to discipline and more laissez-faire than deliberate as a prefaculty development program. We do not know precisely what proportion of current faculty participated in some form of graduate assistantship or teaching assistant training program during graduate study, but the percentage of faculty who have had assistantship experience is likely to be large, particularly among faculty who were students in four-year institutions. Given the expectation of massive replacement of the current faculty over the next twenty-five years, the quality of the graduate assistant experience will be critical. A strong case could be made for graduate schools to share responsibility with departments in assuring that students learn skills of the academic profession as well as the content of their disciplines.

The graduate student is vulnerable and impressionable during the apprenticeship. The effects of socialization "are often very strong, providing an individual with a perspective and orientations that guide a lifetime of academic teaching and research" (Trow, 1977, p. 15). However, not all the role learning is positive; some graduate students reported learning "what not to do" from the negative models their professors provided in teaching, research, and service (Clark and Corcoran, 1983).

Sponsors and Mentors. Sponsor and *mentor* are used interchangeably to describe a person who helps others advance in their careers. The popular "how-to" literature on career advancement assumes that professionals must have either had a sponsor/mentor or been one or must at least be seeking one if they are to succeed. Faculty advisers of graduate students are in a position to model role behavior, set and communicate standards and expectations of advisees' performance, provide career encouragement, help in obtaining a career entry position, and offer other postdegree assistance. We found some differences in adviser behavior that apparently worked to the advantage of highly vital faculty members (Corcoran and Clark, 1984). Particularly instrumental were advisers who provided personal, professional, and direct assistance to advisees, who continued to sponsor their former advisees after degree completion by helping them obtain subsequent positions, by collaborating on research or writing projects, by providing criticism of research and writing, and by acting as a reference and advocate for grant and project applications.

Such individual extensions of help and support can (and should) be offered to the neophyte faculty member by colleagues and administrators and backed up by campus programs in the college, the graduate school, or elsewhere. Beginning a career is a complex, demanding, intense, and frequently stressful process. The novice faculty member must develop a teaching repertoire. The service expectations will probably present unfamiliar and competing demands. The scholarly expectations in research-oriented institutions will require the new faculty member to plan projects, to obtain funds, and to produce results in appropriate form for dissemination during the probationary period. Simultaneously, the entry-level faculty member may be balancing the responsibilities that inhere in the establishment of a family. It is unreasonable to expect new professors to match the productivity and workload of more seasoned faculty members. They may flourish under a lighter teaching and committee assignment.

The setup packages now routinely provided by many institutions to new faculty are important toward meeting basic needs for an office computer, laboratory space and equipment, research assistance, and other aids for establishing the foundations of research and scholarship. Guidance and feedback from colleagues and the department chair are helpful toward removing the mystery surrounding implicit or unclear performance expectations, institutional norms, and reward structures. Likewise, early orientation about campus resources that support the domains of faculty activity is useful. Clearly the pressure on junior faculty today is immense as they "burrow toward tenure" (Bowen and Schuster, 1986, p. 147). Without support and some measure of relief, the probationary period is, for many, a lonely grind.

Renewal and Change in Post-Tenure Faculty

As socialization and career maturation proceed, the individual learns new tasks; establishes relationships with colleagues; clarifies work roles relative to tasks, priorities, and time allocations; evaluates his or her progress in the system; and receives evaluation from others. In addition, conflicting role demands within and beyond the work place are mediated or resolved. If all goes well, a metamorphosis is achieved; the career is well established. The outcome of this process provides the faculty member with a set of internalized role specifications, a sense of satisfaction with work, and a high degree of job involvement and commitment. The faculty member is well on the way to later career stages in which he or she may serve as sponsor, adviser, and organizational leader, as well as in other generative roles. In this idealized version of how a successful career unfolds, the individual is carried along on a smooth escalator ride through the ranks. But the ride may not be smooth or safe in real life, as Becker and Strauss (1956) note:

> The critical passage in some careers lies *near* the beginning . . . when the occupation or institution strongly controls recruitment. In another kind of career, the critical time comes at the end and sometimes very abruptly. Appropriate or strategic timing is called for, to meet opportunity and danger, but the timing becomes vital at different periods in different kinds of careers [pp. 260-261].

Problems of Staging. Some professional careers are relatively unstaged or unstructured. School teaching is an example of a relatively unstaged career, which as a result suffers from lack of an orientation toward the future, difficulty in measuring one's progress against career passage markers, and a relative sense of deprivation among those who are left after colleagues have shifted to other occupations. Staged careers, on the other hand, are oriented toward a future; personal ambitions are successively inspired and satisfied as the individual moves from stage to stage.

Faculty careers are staged at the beginning, but the full professor rank is achieved, on average, in early midlife, with thirty or more years of work life left until retirement.

Midcareer is often a very productive and rewarding phase. However, it can be a time when questions like, Is this all there is? and, What do I want to do with the rest of my life? arise. In particular, the adult development literature warns of problems at this stage such as midlife crisis, plateauing, or getting stuck—as opposed to moving along a career path that assumes an upward trajectory. Midcareer and older faculty, like other professionals, may face obsolescence or depreciation of knowledge and skills. Little attention has been paid to obsolescence as an indicator of faculty vitality compared to that given to obsolescence as a problem for engineers, physicians, and lawyers. Midcareer and older faculty may face the need for career maintenance when the challenges and possibly the satisfactions of tasks have declined.

Midcareer and older faculty may be caught in the awkward circumstances of an institution moving toward a greater emphasis on research and a reward structure shifting toward market-driven compensation for those who are actively publishing. Bowen and Schuster (1986) learned through interviews that both midcareer and senior faculty cohorts at some institutions felt threatened by the new emphasis on research, relegated to subordinate status, resentful toward an ungrateful administration, and suspicious of well-trained young assistant professors (pp. 149–150).

Clark (1987) learned that so great is the tendency toward specialization in academic fields that "tunnel vision may well increase over the course of a university career" (p. 199), and as a result, faculty members may increasingly lose contact with people in other subareas. Counterforces to this trend exist, such as the need to teach in a broader undergraduate curriculum, but extreme specialization could also be a wedge separating department colleagues as careers evolve. And since lines of inquiry can reach dead ends, these faculty may have no escape route without contacts with other areas and colleagues.

Stuckness and Vitality. In addition to the issues of relatively unstaged careers, shifts in institutional missions, and the consequences of specialization, the notion of *stuckness* has received attention because of Kanter's (1977) much-quoted work, *Men and Women of the Corporation,* and her more specific essay on the application of this concept to academic life (1979). She used the term stuckness to describe the situation of people who experience low ceilings in their jobs and who are blocked from movement or lack opportunity in a system where mobility above all means success. In academe this translates to a low promotion rate, a ceiling on opportunities for promotion (movement into the administrative hierarchy is not for everyone), and getting old in one's job.

We learned at a research-oriented university that stuckness or work blockage is not an exceptional experience for faculty members at any stage of their lives (Corcoran and Clark, 1985), nor is it limited to faculty in problematic straits. The most vital and active individuals may well be those who feel most dissatisfied with their jobs because of their sense of frustration in realizing career goals.

Career blocks arise in (1) consistently productive researchers who think they are on a plateau; (2) faculty whose scholarly work was set aside for administrative work and who subsequently find it hard to resume this aspect of a career; (3) faculty who prefer a line of research that is "out of favor" with funding agencies; (4) faculty who see their research as lacking value in the eyes of their colleagues (for example, those whose work deals with the pedagogy of the field); (5) faculty whose work is exceptionally costly in time or travel or other expenses, causing it to be slow to mature; and (6) faculty for whom the shift from the first line of inquiry to another is particularly problematic (for example, starting on the second book in a historical subject, the first being based on the dissertation).

These representative situations revealed the dominant inclination to attribute blockage to situations, including those related to funding, lack of collegial support, lack of graduate student interest, lack of career mobility opportunity, and a general sense that opportunities for advancement were tightening up. While we are unaware of studies focusing on blockages in the teaching role, it is easy to imagine that jadedness could set in after years of teaching routine courses in the curriculum, and that older faculty could feel far removed from the cutting edge of a rapidly changing field (biology, for example).

How are career blockages resolved? Most often, faculty seem to resolve their own blockages with little help from colleagues or institutional sources. Their career socialization, maturity, and problem-solving abilities contribute to an effective resolution. An unknown and costly number of career blockages, however, are not resolved; these faculty remain on a career plateau or begin the process of disengagement from their work by fulfilling minimum requirements and seeking satisfaction elsewhere. Higher education institutions have good reason to devote special attention to the critical career passages of faculty. Established faculty need to review and redefine career goals from time to time. Career consulting and assessment with a counselor or career planning workshop may serve some faculty well. Formal growth-contracting arrangements outlining new goals and development strategies may help others. Discussing intervention with the department chair or dean and targeting resources can be timely and effective. Regardless of the strategy, faculty periodically need to examine their careers and identify new goals and plans.

Post-Tenure Faculty Evaluation

The issue of post-tenure faculty evaluation or review has arisen in the 1980s in part because of the impending elimination of mandatory retirement age for tenured faculty and the associated specter of elderly professors continuing to work even though they are no longer productive. Another impetus is the national movement toward assessing the effectiveness of higher education. According to Licata (1986), much greater attention to faculty evaluation can be expected in the next decade. It will not only be directed to pretenure faculty but will also encompass the evaluation of post-tenure performance and vitality. It is not a popular issue among faculty. "Post-tenure review raises hackles among college faculty and their professional associations" such as the American Association of University Professors (AAUP) (Lee, 1986, p. 106). In the metaphor of psychotherapy as applied to a central but ignored personal reality, it is "the elephant in the room" (Reisman, 1986, p. 74), a nonissue. If the subject is discussed, it is because another university constituency (trustees, administration, legislature) has placed it on the table. We are likely to hear more of it in coming years.

Some of the objection may derive from the belief that periodic, formal evaluation of faculty is unnecessary because aspects of it are essentially in place in promotion reviews, annual salary reviews, the record of success in obtaining external funding for research projects, teaching evaluations, and so forth. Some people are very concerned that post-tenure reviews would bring scant benefit, would be costly, would chill creativity and collegial relationships, and would possibly threaten academic freedom. This is essentially the position of the AAUP. Our purpose in raising the subject in this chapter on faculty renewal and change is not to argue and settle the merits of post-tenure review systems but simply to point out that if thoughtfully developed and provided with ample safeguards, post-tenure evaluation can be a catalyst for faculty development and vitality.

Several principles can be offered to assure that post-tenure reviews support faculty development. (1) The explicit purpose of such reviews should be to provide information that will assist career development. (2) Summative post-tenure review is inconsistent with the philosophy of faculty development and would likely be perceived as a threat to the tenure contract. As such it would be unacceptable to most faculty governance groups. (3) Faculty, of course, must be involved in the design of the program and in the evaluation process itself. (4) The institutional research unit on campus can provide design consultation and expertise in support of the development and implementation of the system, and it should address needs for research on post-tenure review programs. Multiple sources of input to the evaluation process are needed as is agreement on the criteria to be assessed and the standards to be set (Licata, 1986). (5)

A formative post-tenure evaluation should be sensitive to life-course aspects of the faculty career; older faculty will have somewhat different interests, priorities, and plans than faculty who are getting established. (6) Finally, it will serve little developmental purpose to undertake systematic post-tenure reviews and risk engendering cynicism if the linkage between the review process and institutional rewards and resources is not effectively wrought.

Special Issues of Older Faculty

At several points in this chapter we have alluded to concerns about the demography and future quality of the professoriate through the turn of the century. Perspectives on the role of older faculty vary from concerns that stable but stagnant senior professors will remain well beyond age seventy (after 1994) to concerns that unless vigorous senior professors remain available, academe will be hard pressed to meet its staffing needs in areas where personnel shortages are already manifest. Regrettably, insufficient information is available on current retirement decisions in higher education. In the absence of comprehensive national data, some efforts have been made to probe retirement rates within more stratified institutional samples (Lozier and Dooris, 1988–89). In addition to such comparative data, individual institutions need to engage in self-study of the retirement plans of their senior faculty cohorts.

Agenda for Institutional Research. Institutional researchers working with faculty groups and administration should be prepared to develop information for planning the orderly replacement of the faculty and for gauging the need for renewal of faculty in whom institutional investment is substantial. We suggest three major areas of institutional study. The first includes development of demographic data: What is the demographic profile of the faculty by department and college? When do they retire? What do previous retirement age patterns suggest faculty members will do after 1994? What do faculty members themselves plan to do after 1994, and what factors do they feel will affect the timing of their retirement decisions?

The second area deals with institutional policies on tenure, salary, and retirement that could be modified (at least theoretically) in response to the uncapping of mandatory retirement: Should the probationary period be extended? Should a system of post-tenure review be designed and instituted? What are the legal implications and the possible effects on morale and vitality? Should annual salary reviews be more like tenure reviews in their intensity? Should the basis of salary increases be changed to include part base salary and part bonus?

The third area of needed research is on retirement incentives and disincentives: How might the institution move toward a "managed" retirement system that encourages more-productive faculty to remain active longer and less-engaged faculty to retire earlier? What are the costs and benefits of programs based on incentives for early retirement? What types of retirement options should be available? How do amenities and fringe benefits available to retired faculty influence planning and decision making about retirement? Should departments or colleges with problematic age profiles receive special assistance in the form of mortgage or bridge programs on faculty line items? What are promising nontraditional ways of using the talent of retired faculty?

Conclusion

In this chapter we have taken an institutional perspective on issues of faculty renewal and change as they are shaped by late–twentieth century forces in American higher education. We have argued that the faculty career evolves from the graduate student's anticipation of becoming an academic person through a socialization process that extends well into the later years of service as a senior professor. How (and how well) an individual is prepared and inducted into the early career has a bearing on success or failure as these are defined by variable institutional expectations. Planned interventions are vital to the generic needs of faculty as they begin their careers. Graduate schools, in partnerships with departments, could take greater responsibility for preparing doctoral students for the teaching aspect of the faculty career. Active sponsors and mentors for doctoral advisees and junior colleagues (both individually and in cohorts) show promise of benefiting the new faculty member. Novice faculty members have different needs for resources, support, and guidance than midcareer or older faculty.

An awareness of the value of targeted assistance to midcareer faculty is emerging. This assistance includes tangibles that bear directly on faculty working conditions and require monetary resources and intangibles that contribute to morale, satisfaction, vitality, and commitment to the goals of the institution. Institutional researchers could take stock of how well existing arrangements are fostering renewal.

Lack of career staging beyond early middle age, obsolescence, and work blockages are problems typically affecting midcareer and older faculty. We have suggested that faculty members have done relatively well on their own to overcome these structural and individual afflictions. However, post-tenure reviews, if planned and carried out with great care and sensitivity, might serve as a catalyst for the further development of the faculty. The impending end of mandatory retirement will require institutions and collegial governance groups to think in fresh ways about the renewal needs of the oldest members of the professoriate. Managing retirement and faculty replacement after 1994 will challenge institutional researchers to create data bases for planning and policy formulation. Thinking imaginatively about new roles for senior faculty as higher education faces possible personnel shortages is yet another vital issue.

In the past, both faculty and administrators have assumed that faculty renewal was largely the problem of individual members. Now there is a growing understanding that faculty and institutional vitality are intertwined and interactive and that they share responsibilities. Faculty members, as professionals, can and should continue to evaluate their personal needs for renewal and plan on how those needs will be addressed. They will expect to have the major say in what is provided and when, and how well it works. Institutions, as represented by their leaders, will need to invest appropriately in human resource development programs and in strategies that reflect missions and goals. From this synergism, faculty renewal and change are predictable results.

References

Becker, H. S., and Strauss, A. L. "Careers, Personality and Adult Socialization." *American Journal of Sociology*, 1956, *62*, 253–263.

Blackburn, R. T., and Lawrence, J. H. "Aging and the Quality of Faculty Job Performance." *Review of Educational Research*, 1986, *23* (3), 265–290.

Bland, C., and Schmitz, C. C. "Faculty Vitality on Review: Retrospect and Prospect." *Journal of Higher Education*, 1988, *59* (2), 190–224.

Bowen, H. R., and Schuster, J. H. *American Professors: A National Resource Imperiled.* New York: Oxford University Press, 1986.

Centra, J. A. "Types of Faculty Development Programs." *Journal of Higher Education*, 1978, *49*, 151–162.

Clark, B. R. *The Academic Life: Small Worlds, Different Worlds.* Princeton, N.J.: The Carnegie Foundation for the Advancement of Teaching, 1987.

Clark, S. M., and Corcoran, M. "Professional Socialization and Faculty Career Vitality." Paper presented at the American Educational Research Association meeting, Montreal, April 1983.

Clark, S. M., Corcoran, M., and Lewis, D. R. "The Case for an Institutional Perspective on Faculty Development." *Journal of Higher Education*, 1986, *57* (2), 176–195.

Corcoran, M., and Clark, S. M. "Professional Socialization and Contemporary Career Attitudes of Three Faculty Generations." *Research in Higher Education*, 1984, *20* (2), 131–153.

Corcoran, M., and Clark, S. M. "The 'Stuck' Professor: Insights into an Aspect of the Faculty Vitality Issue." In C. Watson (ed.), *The Professoriate: Occupation in Crisis.* Toronto: Ontario Institute for Studies in Higher Education, 1985.

El-Khawas, E. *Campus Trends, 1988.* Higher Education Panel Reports, no. 77. Washington, D.C.: American Council on Education, 1988.

Glaser, B. G. (ed.). *Organizational Careers: A Sourcebook for Theory.* Chicago: Aldine, 1968.

Kanter, R. M. *Men and Women of the Corporation.* New York: Basic Books, 1977.

Kanter, R. M. "Changing the Shape of Work: Reform in Academe." *Current Issues in Higher Education*, 1979, *1*, 3–9.

Lee, B. A. "A New Generation of Tenure Problems: Legal Issues and Institutional

32

Responses." In J. N. Jones and D. P. Semler (eds.), *School Law Update*. Topeka, Kan.: National Organization on Legal Problems of Education, 1986.

Licata, C. M. *Post-Tenure Faculty Evaluation: Threat or Opportunity?* ASHE-ERIC Higher Education Research Report, no. 1. Washington, D.C.: Association for the Study of Higher Education, 1986.

Lortie, D. C. *Schoolteacher: A Sociological Study*. Chicago: University of Chicago Press, 1975.

Lozier, G. L., and Dooris, M. J. "Elimination of Mandatory Retirement: Anticipating Faculty Response." *Planning for Higher Education*, 1988–89, *17* (2), 1–14.

Reisman, B. "Performance Evaluation for Tenured Faculty: Issues and Research." *Liberal Education*, 1986, *72* (1), 73–87.

Rice, R. E., and Austin, A. E. "High Faculty Morale: What Exemplary Colleges Do Right." *Change*, March/April 1988, 50–58.

Shein, E. H. "Organizational Socialization." *Industrial Management Review*, 1968, *2*, 37–45.

Trow, M. "Departments as Contexts for Teaching and Learning." In D. E. McHenry and Associates (eds.), *Academic Departments: Problems, Variations, and Alternatives*. San Francisco: Jossey-Bass, 1977.

Shirley M. Clark is professor of education and sociology at the University of Minnesota. She is acting provost of the Twin Cities campus and vice-president for academic affairs for 1988–89.

Mary E. Corcoran is professor emeritus of higher education and educational psychology at the University of Minnesota, where she works for the concerns of retired faculty.

The practical and policy implications of employing part-time, temporary, and non-tenure track faculty are explored.

Creative Staffing: Problems and Opportunities

David W. Leslie

Traditional tenure track faculty appointments are becoming less common as conditions in the profession change and as universities and colleges take on new roles and functions. This statement is not meant to advocate the abolition of tenure; it is rather meant to reflect existing conditions in the profession and among institutions of postsecondary education. One condition, the aging of the professoriate, has produced a tightening in the supply of open tenure lines and a concomitant reduction in the rate of hiring junior, tenure track faculty.

The constraints of an aging cohort of tenured faculty are only part of the picture. Although some fields are oversupplied with faculty, others are undersupplied. Fields like business and engineering are experiencing a clear and critical shortage of new Ph.D.'s willing to forgo high salaries in the private sector for the intangible rewards of professorships and the lengthy uncertainty associated with the quest for tenure.

Other pressures point to change in the tenure system, too. Women in increasing numbers are achieving terminal academic and professional degrees—many in nontraditional fields. Their concerns encompass deci-

The author gratefully acknowledges the comments of James Parry, director of human resources for the State University System of Florida.

G. G. Lozier and M. J. Dooris (eds.). *Managing Faculty Resources.*
New Directions for Institutional Research, no. 63. San Francisco: Jossey-Bass, Fall 1989.

sions about both career and family. The expression of their professional interests may require restructuring an academic personnel system designed at a time when men (or single women) occupied virtually all faculty slots at most institutions.

The substance of many academic fields is changing, too. Trends in schools of education, for example, favor appointment of more "clinical" faculty—particularly experienced schoolteachers who can serve as role models and mentors to aspiring educators. The increasing inclusion in university settings of fields previously considered primarily vocational (such as nursing and physical therapy) also places pressure on traditional assumptions about faculty roles.

Whatever the causes of increasing numbers of nontraditional, non–tenure track appointments, the numbers are undeniable. Community colleges often employ well over half of their faculty in part-time, temporary, or adjunct positions. A recent analysis of appointments in the California State University system documents the increasing rate of non–tenure track appointments and concludes:

> The loss of tenured faculty and use of part-time faculty in the California State University has resulted from conditions familiar to other higher education institutions: (1) the difficulty in filling tenure track positions in schools of business and engineering when faculty can obtain higher paying jobs in industry; (2) "tenuring in" of departments in humanities and social sciences because of shifts in student enrollments; and (3) the oversupply of holders of the Ph.D. degree in fields such as history, English, foreign languages, anthropology, and . . . chemistry and biological sciences [Pollack, 1986, pp. 21–22].

The best available count from the Department of Education's Center for Education Statistics suggests that just over one-third of all faculty in postsecondary institutions are now in part-time positions. These numbers are far higher in community colleges and far lower in other sectors, but the rule is extreme variability; some institutions staff virtually all of their instructional positions with part-time faculty while others use virtually none at all.

Several major reports have categorically opposed employment of non–tenure track faculty. *Involvement in Learning*, issued in 1984 by a National Institute of Education study group, recommended that "academic administrators should consolidate as many part-time teaching lines into as many full-time positions as possible" (National Institute of Education, 1984, p. 36). Howard Bowen and Jack Schuster, in their landmark work *American Professors: A National Resource Imperiled* (1986), also advocated reducing the share of instruction borne by part-time faculty. Policy positions opposing the employment of part-time faculty have been issued by the

American Association of University Professors, the National Education Association, and the Canadian Association of University Teachers ("Senior Appointments . . . ," 1987; National Education Association, 1988).

Policy constraints notwithstanding, postsecondary institutions have been responsive to their own needs for new kinds of faculty appointments. They have also been willing to accommodate the individual needs of faculty who have personal and professional commitments that either prevent traditional pursuit of tenure track appointments or require such pursuit to be delayed or stretched out.

Of necessity most institutions employ at least some part-time or adjunct faculty, who accept less-than-full-time positions to teach. Many institutions also use an array of nontraditional appointments to achieve a balance between individual and institutional interests. These include temporary, visiting, courtesy, joint, interdisciplinary, and a variety of other appointments. The common denominators are threefold:

1. *Noncontinuous funding sources,* meaning that the positions are not budgeted and must be funded from sources that support temporary employees, from the salary savings generated by vacated (open) lines, or from soft-money sources.

2. *Term appointments,* meaning that there is a definite limit to the time individuals may serve. By necessity, most terms are short and seldom exceed a semester or a year.

3. *Specified assignments,* meaning that individuals are hired for a particular assignment, such as teaching one specific course. Duties are limited by the terms of the contract.

Experiments have begun with still newer kinds of appointments. For example, dual-career couples may share a single faculty position. In some cases single positions are shared by unrelated individuals whose personal lives require a limited professional commitment. Other institutions have experimented with phased retirement programs that allow faculty to receive retirement benefits earlier in exchange for a reduced teaching assignment.

The rationales for using nontraditional, non–tenure track appointments are both economic and academic. Converting budgeted lines to flexible appointments allows institutions to adapt more rapidly to changing conditions than they can when those lines are committed to tenured faculty. Using flexible lines allows an institution to search for and utilize expertise that may be required only cyclically or periodically in evolving academic and professional programs.

Problems with Nontraditional Appointments

Rationales for using nontraditional appointments to the contrary, significant problems arise in freely utilizing part-time, non–tenure track faculty.

Management Overhead. Managing this work force and displacing the burdens of many routine, noninstructional activities onto full-time faculty, for example, add hidden cost. Faculty serving in these positions are usually appointed by departments without higher-level review. The contracts are individually (often verbally) consummated outside the normal rules and regulations governing faculty personnel; controls and standards are not applied. Many nonstandard appointments do not show up in whatever faculty appointment data the institution collects. Institutions using nontraditional appointments may not know who is employed at the institution for what reasons and at what cost.

Use of part-time and adjunct faculty often means high turnover. Many new instructors are likely to be engaged in any given semester. As with all new personnel, start-up costs are heavy. Providing library cards, orienting people in procedure, spending time answering questions, and assuring an adequate level of knowledge about routine matters incur the minimal and obvious costs. Some enlightened institutions go further and provide formal orientation sessions and mentors for part-time faculty.

Seldom counted as a cost in employing part-time faculty is the continuing need to search and recruit. Someone, usually a department head, must manage the continuous turnover by assuring new hires to fill vacated positions. Substantial time may be allocated to this work in a large department employing many part-timers.

Part-time faculty usually do not carry the full array of responsibilities assumed by full-time faculty. Departments and programs require coordination and cooperative decision making, reflected in committee work and institutional service normally assignable as costs to faculty workload accounts. No less cooperative decision making, planning, coordination, and overall service may be required when large numbers of adjuncts are employed; to the contrary, it may become more difficult and time-consuming to coordinate academic programs under these circumstances. The full-time faculty, often the more senior (and therefore more costly) faculty, necessarily assume this work, which drives up the rate of overhead (service functions performed by faculty) in proportion to their average salary.

Other services, like advising students, developing new courses, and supervising internships or apprenticeships at off-campus sites are also rendered more expensive, for the same reasons. Of course, a major hidden cost in loading such services onto full-time faculty lies in the de facto reduction in their direct teaching. Where the use of part-time faculty is proportionately high, full-time faculty may become quasi-administrators with minimal teaching assignments. Although the impact on quality is not strictly measurable, many argue that the displacement of full-time faculty from instruction is harmful and that teaching is devalued by delegating a disproportionate amount to temporary or part-time faculty.

From the viewpoint of institutional cost, using more part-time faculty may drive the accountable cost of instruction down, but it concomitantly drives the cost of other institutional functions up. The alternative is to perform all noninstructional functions at minimal levels—for example, by opting not to provide responsible levels of student advising. At such junctures the argument that the extensive use of part-time faculty affects quality gains force.

Using alternative kinds of faculty appointments does not always mean cost savings. If maintaining quality—or improving it—is accepted as a policy objective, then the management overhead inherent in relying on large numbers of part-time faculty should be carefully analyzed.

Exploitation. Anecdotal evidence is abundant that institutions exploit the surplus of new Ph.D.'s in certain fields (the humanities, in particular) to find cheap, temporary labor. In some parts of the country, especially large metropolitan areas, a fair number of "gypsy" faculty teach part-time at several institutions simultaneously.

Young people who have invested heavily in a graduate degree and who aspire to a teaching career sometimes take years of extraordinary risk by accepting temporary employment on a term-to-term basis in the hope that their good work will result in access to tenure track positions. They work at low pay, without annual raises, and without access to essential benefits like health and group life insurance. They are almost certainly disenfranchised in any faculty bargaining unit and in regular institutional and departmental governance. They have minimal access to institutional resources like secretarial support, telephones, and office space and equipment.

The social marginality and alienation experienced by this group can have important effects. Several bargaining units of part-time faculty have been formed at major universities in the past few years, including Rutgers University, the University of California, and the University of Maine (Maitland, 1987). The Canadian experience is also instructive. Part-time faculty there have formed a national union, the Canadian Union of Educational Workers. Its chapters have struck several institutions in Quebec and have shown a militance that far exceeds anything seen to date in the United States (Gersón, 1987).

Creating a Two-Tiered Profession. The extensive use of part-time and temporary non–tenure track appointments will likely lead to a two-tiered profession. The "haves" will enjoy the protections of tenure and the economic benefits traditionally provided to full-time faculty. The "have nots" will wander from job to job, accepting low pay, insecurity, lack of benefits, and lack of access to offices, services, laboratories, libraries, and other requisites of a professional working environment.

Two further dangers exist in tiering. The first is that some academic fields will be affected profoundly while others will not be affected at all.

Specifically, the soft fields of humanities and the social sciences are now experiencing a surplus in the faculty marketplace. Business and engineering, on the other hand, sometimes find it impossible to fill an open line for years because the available talent opts for high salaries in the private sector. To recruit faculty in the latter fields, institutions will have to make appointments as attractive (and as expensive) as possible. The resources, already scarce, will have to come from areas in which faculty can be hired more cheaply. Thus, the institution will be tempted to make more temporary and part-time non–tenure track appointments in some fields while using the saved resources to make tenure track appointments elsewhere.

The result is not just a two-tiered profession but one that is creating imbalances among disciplines. If this practice continues for years, several results are predictable. Disciplines with economic leverage will accumulate power. In time they will have a preponderance of tenured and senior faculty in their ranks and will be able to dominate institutional governance mechanisms. The essence of the institution may be altered by the new balance of seniority and by the coloring of decision making.

Another effect of tiering may lead to similar results. Some disciplines, by over-reliance on non–tenure track faculty, may become relatively disenfranchised from opportunities for research and scholarship. If humanities and social science departments, for example, begin to staff with non–tenure track teachers, the long-term output of sound research in these fields may be skewed. If temporary and part-time faculty do not receive research assignments and if they constitute larger proportions of the staff in certain fields, what will be the impact on scholarship in those fields?

Tiering may also have a serious effect on affirmative action. The fields in which temporary and part-time positions may become most common are just the fields in which women and minorities are most represented. Without careful monitoring, disproportionate numbers of women and minorities could be hired into positions that do not lead to advancement and that result in great salary disparities.

Strengthening Programs with Creative Appointments

Systematic use of creative appointments may generate hidden overhead and inequities that are destructive of faculty morale and productivity and that diminish quality in academic programs. But selective use of part-time and non–tenure track appointments may provide leverage for improving programs and enhancing quality. The rationale for making such appointments may vary considerably from time to time and from one institution to another. The key is to avoid making institutionwide use of part-time faculty a budgetary rule. It may be a de facto necessity, but it should not become a permanent addiction without some effort to rationalize separately each such appointment.

Gaining Access to Scarce Expertise. Faculty with the right kind of expertise are not always available, particularly to small rural institutions. As student demand and program cycles move through phases, institutions may need to hire a particular kind of person for a short term or for an intermittent demand. Every three years, for example, a seminar on monetary theory may be offered in a department with no permanent monetarist. The need may be met locally, or it may become an opportunity for the department to make a visiting appointment.

Institutions in some major metropolitan areas, on the other hand, have turned average programs into world-class programs by tapping an array of talent available in the community. New York is rich in artistic talent; Washington, in public affairs; Chicago, in finance and law; Boston, in science and engineering. Colleges and universities in such areas frequently tap high-level talent pools to bring outstanding visiting faculty to their campuses.

In either situation—that of scarce or abundant expertise—the decision to staff with adjunct or temporary appointments is not driven by economics. Theoretically, an institution seeking scarce expertise will pay a premium to get what is needed. Bringing students into contact with new ideas and perspectives from exceptionally qualified professionals is worth whatever premium one might have to pay for such talent. In reality, however, such premiums are not necessarily demanded by potential faculty. Those with already high salaries or lucrative private practices sometimes decline to be paid, because the relatively small amount they will receive is taxed at a high marginal rate. They may want to teach for personal or professional reasons and base their negotiating position on a mixture of intrinsic and extrinsic rewards—salary is often a minor consideration. From a policy standpoint, the institution should be willing to pay a high premium to enhance quality; from a practical standpoint, it might both enhance quality and save money by appointing an adjunct or part-time professor, but the economic advantage is purely serendipitous.

Managing Student Demand. Student demand is notoriously cyclical. Engineering and business are "up" today; education shows signs of being "up" in the near future. Enrollment in medicine is falling at a rate one could scarcely have predicted in the recent past.

Education provides a fine case in point. Nationally, enrollment in education today is about half of what it was in the early 1970s. Many colleges of education have undergone a massive retrenchment, experiencing staff reductions reflective of declining student interest. More recently a resurgence of interest has been recorded, and the first wave of increasing enrollment is appearing in undergraduate programs. These new students are likely to be aspiring teachers, however, and not potential administrators, counselors, or other specialists. The retrenchment of staff in colleges of education has not generally been strategic; faculty who have survived the retrenchment are almost certainly not those with expertise and interest in teacher education. Instead, they earned tenure at a time when research and specialization had become au courant in colleges of education. They are unlikely to show an intense interest in the surging demand for teacher training.

Thus, colleges of education have to face a demand for courses with a faculty resource that is out of phase with that demand. Specialized graduate faculty will be teaching expensive, small classes; large numbers of students will request sections of teacher preparation courses that cannot be staffed. The imbalance has to be met and probably should be met, at least in part, with adjunct, clinical, and temporary faculty.

This is a case, however, in which creative staffing is a temporary and not a strategic solution. The department or college has to decide on an appropriate long-term commitment to teacher education. In Florida, the board of regents has adopted a policy that will require doubling the capacity for new-teacher production in five years. Some of that capacity may be developed by encouraging more potential teachers to complete arts and sciences majors. But some will undoubtedly have to be met by re-allocating existing and occupied lines within colleges of education. The immediate program need, however, is for temporary faculty to absorb rapidly growing enrollment until such re-allocation can be accomplished. Reliance on temporaries and adjuncts in this case should be viewed as a stopgap and not as a long-term solution. Strategically, the problem is to project long-term demand for teacher preparation, the content of anticipated curricula in areas of expanded demand, and the nature of faculty expertise required for needed programs.

Gaining Access to Current Knowledge and Practice. In many professional fields, practice develops ahead of theory. This seems especially true in technical fields, where business and industry adopt new technology faster than limited equipment budgets will permit in institutions of higher education. For professional training to match the curve of employers' expectations, state-of-the-art practice must be taught. Such training programs must include adjunct and clinical faculty who provide access to knowledge, practice, and even equipment that students will need if they are to be marketable.

Training marketable graduates is a permanent, long-term need in many program areas, particularly those preparing technicians. Planning would rest on the assumption that adjuncts are integral to program quality, currency, and legitimacy and that they form a strategic resource in selected programs.

Forming Links with Employers and the Professional Community. Just as it is important for students to be exposed to the state of the art in technical practice, so is it important for potential employers to be exposed to students.

Finding ways to expand dialogue between practitioners and academics is also useful. To bring corporate executives, partners in professional firms, government officials, school superintendents, artists, ambassadors, social activists, and others to the campus is to open students to new experiences, ideas, and practices. If visiting faculty can also be productively engaged in dialogue with permanent faculty on professional matters, both sides will benefit. Visiting professionals benefit by having access to new theory and ideas; faculty benefit by learning how practitioners use new knowledge, solve problems, and generate new questions for research.

These linkages, if they include students in the process, can be highly productive for all sides. Knowledge, insight, and practical wisdom pass from one source to another in the spirit of a learning community, and students' job prospects are enhanced.

Enhancing Morale. In a time of changing roles, many prospective academics choose not to work full time. Some prefer to phase into retirement by reducing their work load. Others wish to place a temporary or permanent emphasis on family responsibilities. Many teach for altruistic reasons and enjoy the intrinsic rewards of contact with young minds but do not wish to engage in a full-time academic career. Flexible appointment terms can satisfy many of these motives and can result in the engagement of talented teachers. Satisfaction of personal motives to work less than full time is an important benefit and morale boost for those who choose adjunct or reduced-load appointments.

Increasing Visibility and Credibility. Appointing prominent professionals to adjunct positions—assuming academic and other qualifications are in order—can bring positive public notice to an institution. This is not to advocate either sham appointments or the shameless milking of someone's good name for undeserved benefit. But bona fide appointment of people with professional stature to adjunct positions can enhance the image and visibility of a program or department.

Providing Opportunity and Investing in the Future. Some fields are overcrowded with young, qualified Ph.D.'s. Despite a current lack of academic openings, possible shortages in the 1990s and later may mean that institutions will have to search harder than ever to find the right people. Meanwhile the present surplus of Ph.D.'s may forsake academia altogether and become a lost generation. Their skills will erode and their interest in scholarly work decline. It is sometimes suggested that fractional or other nontraditional appointments—if full-time appointments are not possible—are one way to keep the energies and interests of this generation in frontier scholarship and teaching. The danger, however, is that this salvage mentality could turn into exploitation. Great care and candor is needed in reaching understandings with those appointed to temporary positions if the positions bring hope of more permanent appointments in the future.

These temporary appointments may be viewed as institutional investments in the future viability of disciplines or fields of study; the institution would want those appointed to consider their own future with one of its departments. Such appointments would not be made for reasons of economy or convenience. The institution would want to invest in the long-term development of the person's professional standing, knowledge, and skill. It would therefore want to provide for a rounded experience, including opportunities for research and professional accomplishment, opportunities to participate in departmental affairs and develop new courses, and access to the full range of benefits available to full-time tenure track faculty.

An alternative to temporary staffing is "stockpiling." Institutions learning of opportunities to hire faculty with scarce talents may mortgage lines on which they anticipate vacancies in the near future to hire potential stars when they are available. This aggressive strategy requires a clear sense of where specific programs are headed, lest hiring a star for the sake of having a star skews priorities and introduces conflict over goals and directions. On the other hand, it can be opportunism at its best and may pay long-term dividends on the investment.

Policy Issues in Creative Staffing

Rules and Standards. One of the principles underlying creative staffing is the need to individualize employment terms. One of the dangers here is that the institution will treat some people arbitrarily and capriciously or, worse, that it will be discriminatory. Denial of due process or equal protection of the law is the risk. Therefore, some balance must be sought.

Although it is not often done, an institution might consider establishing general policy guidelines for different classes of nontraditional appointments. The State University System of Florida, for example, has established a set of rules governing employment of "service professors," who opt for reduced appointments through a period of phased retirement. Other classes of nontraditional appointment could also be handled with separate rules. Administering a proliferation of rules is burdensome, but assuming the risk of random individual agreements—the common practice—may be more so.

Collective Bargaining. Part-time faculty are showing increased interest in forming separate collective bargaining units. The Canadian experience cited earlier suggests that this interest can become—under objective deprivation and inequity in employment conditions—a serious and militant movement. This issue merits a separate treatment at length.

Institutions with a substantial number of part-timers will want to consider a general strategy regarding bargaining unit composition. Often, some part-timers are included in the full-time faculty unit. But if a clear distinction between part- and full-time faculty can be made in terms and conditions of employment and of "interest," then a separate unit may be created by the labor board. Given that most faculty, by virtue of federal or state law, have a right to choose a bargaining agent, the only open question is how the unit is composed. Who is "in" and who is "out" lays the groundwork for how the future development of policies governing the use of part-time faculty will be conducted: (a) at the bargaining table with full-time faculty; (b) at the bargaining table with part-time faculty; or (c) separately from any collective bargaining process.

Equity. Faculty in nontraditional appointments are often concerned about equity. They typically receive minimal compensation, few or no benefits, and severely limited access to university services, and they are excluded from governance. Sometimes this is of little or no concern; some part-time faculty do not want anything more than the opportunity to teach. Others depend on these jobs for all of their income and security. The present system allows capricious treatment of less-than-full-time faculty. Some are exploited because they are vulnerable; some are treated well whether they need it or not.

If an institution knows it will systematically and continuously employ temporary or part-time faculty, it may want to analyze its current patterns and the equity implications. For example, are temporary appointments in engineering typically different than those in English? On what terms do they differ? Are there grounds for an equity complaint? (A fuller discussion of equity issues is presented in Chapter Four.)

Faculty Resource Management. Most institutions keep intricate data on their full-time faculty, but comparatively few know anything about their part-time faculty. How many part-time staff do what kinds of teaching, research, or service and in which departments? What are they paid? How do they fit into departmental plans? Are departments using them because they cannot afford full-time faculty or find them? Or are other reasons in play? What does the use of part-time faculty imply for the institution as a whole? Are they being employed strategically and to good effect, or are they being exploited as a stopgap solution to financial stress? Does the use of large numbers of part-time faculty suggest a failure to make strategic choices? Is the institution simply spreading scarce resources over all existing programs in a mindless attempt to be all things to all people? Should it consolidate part-time positions into full-time positions? What are the consequences of continuing existing staffing patterns? Of changing them in strategic ways? Institutional researchers can lay the groundwork for answering such questions by developing staffing profiles that include detailed analyses of the part-time faculty resource.

Conclusion

Creative staffing is a temptation forced on many institutions by budgetary constraints. Capitalizing on opportunities while saving scarce resources provides the motive to appoint faculty to part-time, adjunct, and non-tenure track positions. The current policy debate over using such positions assumes that the quality of education will be negatively impacted if too many temporary faculty are hired.

I have argued that there are many consequences of using creative faculty appointments but that not all are negative; in some cases temporary appointments may demonstrably strengthen programs. The deeper hazards lie in the long-term impact on the structure and character of the academic profession. If temporary appointments are used carefully and for clearly educational (as opposed to merely budgetary) reasons, the benefits can be substantial.

To realize these benefits, institutional policy must assure fair, equitable, and appropriate terms of employment for individuals whose interests may differ substantially from those of faculty in traditional positions. The academic community faces a considerable challenge in legitimizing the practice of creative staffing, but most institutions now make such appointments. They might well consider how the terms and conditions under which temporary and nontraditional appointments are made can contribute to the educational quality of academic programs.

References

Bowen, H., and Schuster, J. *American Professors: A National Resource Imperiled.* New York: Oxford University Press, 1986.

Gersón, M. "Part-Time Teachers Strike at U. of Quebec at Montreal." *Chronicle of Higher Education,* April 8, 1987, p. 41.

Maitland, C. "Temporary Faculty and Collective Bargaining in Higher Education in California." *Journal of Collective Negotiations in the Public Sector,* 1987, *16* (3), 233–258.

National Education Association. *To Promote Academic Justice and Excellence: Report and Recommendations on Part-Time, Temporary, and Nontenure Track Faculty Appointments.* Washington, D.C.: National Education Association, 1988.

National Institute of Education. *Involvement in Learning: Realizing the Potential of American Higher Education.* Washington, D.C.: National Institute of Education, U.S. Department of Education, 1984.

Pollack, J. S. "The Erosion of Tenure in the California State University." *Academe,* 1986, *72* (1), 19–25.

"Senior Appointments with Reduced Loads." *Academe,* 1987, *73* (4), 50.

David W. Leslie is professor and director of the Institute for Studies in Higher Education at Florida State University.

The task of building the future professoriate can be facilitated by giving attention to important dimensions of affirmative action.

The Status of Women and Minorities in the Professoriate: The Role of Affirmative Action and Equity

Kathryn M. Moore, Michael P. Johnson

We begin this discussion with a proposition: "Management is the active entrepreneurial shaping of an organization's or institution's future life" (Keller, 1982, p. 4). Human resource management must be concerned with building toward a desired future for the institution. An important aspect of that future concerns the composition of the faculty—the mix of disciplines, ranks, ages, sexes, and minorities—that will be present to achieve the educational missions of the institution. In the latter years of

A June 1989 U.S. Supreme Court decision (*Martin* v. *Wilks*) has raised questions about the role of affirmative action in the hiring of underrepresented groups. At this time, the full impact of that decision cannot be assessed; however, the policy and procedural initiatives suggested by this chapter continue to offer sound guidance in promoting diversity on our campuses—*Editors.*

G. G. Lozier and M. J. Dooris (eds.). *Managing Faculty Resources.*
New Directions for Institutional Research, no. 63. San Francisco: Jossey-Bass, Fall 1989.

the twentieth century it seems clear that greater diversity among the faculty is both desirable and demanded.

Greater diversity is desirable because the population of the nation is increasingly diverse, because problems and our approaches to them are complex and require the efforts of many kinds of expertise, and because a multicultural work place is becoming the norm for all sectors of society, higher education included. Diversity is also demanded by the populations of students who enter our institutions, by the taxpayers who support, in one form or another, all of our institutions, and by the ideals of the nation as they have evolved over our history in law, precedent, and practice.

This chapter will show how campus leaders, including institutional research professionals, can assist in building the professoriate by giving attention to the important dimensions of affirmative action that have been developed since 1972. To do this we will provide a brief background of the development of affirmative action policy and practice; then we will present a model of faculty hiring and retention and show how the model can be used to establish internal affirmative action targets; and finally, we will consider means to improve the record in affirmative action and equity, many of which enlist the assistance and expertise of institutional research professionals.

Although our discussion focuses on the hiring, retention, and advancement of women and racial and ethnic minorities, we must note that affirmative action policy covers other under-represented groups, such as disabled persons and veterans. We are confident that this discussion will be relevant to these other groups in many respects and that their members will benefit if our suggestions are followed. The primary goal is to improve and enhance the quality of that professoriate by incorporating a greater diversity of talent and experience from all groups.

Development of Affirmative Action Policies and Procedures

Colleges and universities are obligated to avoid discrimination against employees and applicants for employment on the basis of race, color, religion, sex, national origin, veteran status, or handicap. The principal sources of this obligation are the Fourteenth Amendment to the United States Constitution (the equal protection clause); federal statutes, including the Civil Rights Act of 1964, especially Title VII, Title IX of the Education Amendments of 1972, the Equal Pay Act of 1963, and Section 504 of the Vocational Rehabilitation Act of 1973; and Executive Order 11246 as amended by Executive Orders 11375 and 12086. In some states, similar responsibilities are imposed by state statute. Most of these obligations became applicable to colleges and universities in 1972. "Since then, it is reasonably clear that the obligations of colleges and universities to avoid discriminating against employees and/or applicants for employment because of their sex [and other protected characteristics] are approximately the same as those of any other employer" (Lindgren, Ota, Zirkel, and Gieson, 1984, p. 27).

Subsequent to the passage of Title VII in 1964 and issuance of the executive order, the federal government promulgated a set of guidelines to be followed in implementing affirmative action in educational institutions. They apply to all educational institutions with a federal contract of over $100,000 and with over one hundred employees. A critical component in the guidelines is the distinction between nondiscrimination and affirmative action. Nondiscrimination is defined as "the elimination of all existing discriminatory conditions, whether purposeful or inadvertent," on the basis of race, color, religion, national origin, or sex (Carnegie Commission on Higher Education, 1975, p. 116). Affirmative action goes further by requiring assurance of "employment neutrality" through deliberate and positive efforts on the part of institutions to rectify existing inequities that have resulted from past discrimination (Carnegie Commission on Higher Education, 1973).

To establish whether such inequities exist and to what extent, a job analysis must be undertaken to determine the "underutilization" of women, minorities, and other protected classes of employees. Various data sources are available to help institutions determine availability and to calculate the percentage underutilization of available talent from both local and national employment pools. On the basis of job analyses for all categories of employees, not simply faculty, each institution must prepare an affirmative action plan that sets numerical goals consistent with available labor pools and with projected turnover in employment, and that specifies a timetable for improving the situation. The numerical goals are targets of desired achievement, not quotas that must be met. The institution is responsible for setting the criteria it will use for hiring, promotion, and retention. It must make them "reasonable and explicit" and widely available to employees and applicants. Individual departments or units within the institution must document reasons for employment decisions and record the representation of members of the protected categories at various stages of the employment process (Carnegie Commission on Higher Education, 1973; Lindgren, Ota, Zirkel, and Gieson, 1984; Vetter and Babco, 1987).

In addition, the institution must establish a central office to audit and monitor the overall operation of the process and to make a formal annual report to the Department of Labor, Office of Federal Contract Compliance, on the progress of its affirmative action plan and program. The Department of Labor (DOL) as well as other federal agencies are empowered to examine the relevant documents to determine whether the institution has been making "good faith" efforts to implement its plan.

Compliance reviews may be initiated by DOL or other federal agencies at any time. Such agencies can request delays in awarding federal contracts (occasionally pursued), or they can recommend denials or terminations of contracts (seldom initiated).

Department of Labor guidelines also require or recommend other important steps for institutions to incorporate in their plans and actions. Among these are the following:

1. Identify and recruit protected groups by using search committees that include representatives of these groups, by drawing on data provided by women's and minorities' groups and disciplinary and professional associations, by advertising openings through channels that will reach women and minorities, and by stating in such advertising that the institutions are equal opportunity employers;
2. Ensure that salaries are based on qualifications and merit rather than on ascriptive qualities;
3. Abolish antinepotism rules;
4. Reconsider any policies that prohibit a department from hiring its own graduate students, since these policies have often worked to the disadvantage of women and minorities;
5. See that maternity leaves are granted to women and that parental leaves for child rearing are granted to both sexes;
6. Develop sound internal grievance procedures; and
7. Prepare and disseminate a written policy of nondiscrimination and publish the affirmative action plan (adapted from Carnegie Commission, 1973).

Since 1972 numerous important developments have occurred as the result of litigation, procedural clarifications, and new legislation. For example, the Equal Employment Opportunity Commission (EEOC) published guidelines concerning sexual harassment. The Pregnancy Discrimination Act of 1978 was passed by Congress. The Supreme Court interpreted Title VII as forbidding employers' sponsorship of insurance and retirement programs based on sex-based actuarial tables. Lower courts have increasingly and consistently approved the permissibility of affirmative action programs developed under the executive order against both equal protection and Title VII challenges. Recently lower courts have supported the right of academic plaintiffs, under carefully prescribed circumstances, to gain access to the content of confidential peer-review files and even tenure votes, and have begun to permit and lend credence to statistical evidence in discrimination cases (Lindgren, Ota, Zirkel, and Gieson, 1984; Hendrickson and Lee, 1983; LaNoue and Lee, 1987; Lester, 1974). Litigation continues to challenge and refine the legal bases of affirmative action.

Even as these changes occur, similar structures and processes have been established in most higher education institutions. As a result, most institutions have designated one or more officials to be responsible for overseeing the preparation and operation of the affirmative action plan. These persons typically are not housed in the institutional research area, but they often must rely heavily on the information generated by institutional research to prepare the plan, to make the annual report, and to monitor progress on goals throughout the institution and across time, including promotion, tenure, and salary equity matters.

In many cases the vagaries and complexities of faculty appointments and other employment categories make the task rather more complex than providing simple numeric counts. For example, analyses of salary equity, a component of a full affirmative action plan, have advanced to a sophisticated level of statistical manipulation on many campuses. Compliance reviews place another set of demands for institutional information, often more detailed and penetrating than the institution-wide report. Litigation, if it occurs, also draws heavily on institutional information. On the plus side, some have asserted that if they have done nothing else, the requirements of affirmative action reporting have been the cause for upgrading and refining institutional data bases in ways no other comparable federal regulations (apart from financial aid) have accomplished. On the down side, the burden for preparing and disseminating all this information is a large but often hidden cost in administering institutions today.

Given nearly two decades of legislative, judicial, administrative, and professional activity, one might assume substantial improvements have been achieved in the numerical representation of individuals from protected classes. But such an expectation would be unwarranted. A brief review of recent data on the number of women and minority faculty employed in higher education since 1972 indicates that the results have not matched the effort.

Current Status of Affirmative Action Efforts

According to several studies, the proportion of all full-time faculty who are women has grown over the last thirteen years from 22.3 percent in 1972 to 27.5 percent in 1985 (Vetter and Babco, 1987; Etaugh, 1984); however, it has yet to regain the 29-percent mark established in 1929 (Finkelstein, 1984). Women are not equally represented across disciplines or types of institutions. They continue to be clustered in a relatively small number of academic fields such as English, foreign languages, nursing, home economics, fine arts, and library science (Vetter and Babco, 1987; Gappa and Uehling, 1979). With strong national interest in increasing the number of women in science and engineering, their representation here increased from 14.7 to 21.1 percent between 1974 and 1985 (Vetter and Babco, 1987; Widnall, 1988), but the gains have occurred in the lower ranks and only in certain fields.

Women are disproportionately located in community colleges (37.6 percent) and at four-year colleges (29.3 percent) (Vetter and Babco, 1987). They are under-represented at universities, with an overall representation of 20.0 percent, but at the major research universities the percentage is even lower (National Center for Education Statistics, as reported by Vetter and Babco, 1987). Moreover, women advance through the academic ranks more slowly than men and tend to be concentrated in the lower ranks. This situation has remained virtually unchanged over the last decade. More women have joined the instructor and assistant professor ranks, but the number who pass the tenure hurdle and achieve associate and full professor status remains low. In 1985 women accounted for 11.4 percent of full professors, an increase of about 2 percent since 1972 (Vetter and Babco, 1987).

Salary differentials reflect these essential structural features nationally. Women are clustered in the lower ranks, the lower-paid academic disciplines, and in the lesser-status institutions. After nearly two decades, women are still paid less than their male counterparts at every rank, across every discipline, and in all types of institutions (Koch, 1982). According to Bowen and Schuster (1986): "In 1976–77 the overall salaries of women were about 94 percent of those of men of comparable academic rank . . . By 1983–84 some retrogression appears to have occurred at all three ranks. . . . from a low of 89.1 percent at the full professor rank to 93.9 percent at the assistant professor rank" (p. 103). In *The Chronicle of Higher Education*, McMillen (1987) reported that women's average salaries were 88 percent of men's. This "retrogression" is attributed at least in part to the effect of recent increased hirings and promotions of women, which has tended to increase their presence in the lower-paying ranges of all ranks (Bowen and Schuster, 1986). Salary discrepancies are greatest for full professors regardless of discipline, but men's and women's salaries also vary by institution type, with greater differences in the private sector than in the public sector. Salary differentials between men and women are greatest in the universities and private institutions, where women are least represented, and smallest in institutions with the greatest proportion of women, such as two-year colleges and public institutions, generally (Vetter and Babco, 1987).

Current information on minority representation is perhaps even more discouraging. According to various reports, the number of blacks holding faculty appointments has risen only slightly since the latter half of the seventies (Bowen and Schuster, 1986). Indeed, fewer black scholars entered the professorial ranks in 1979 than in 1975 (Harvey and Scott-Jones, 1985; Reed, 1983; Sandoval, 1983). Harvey and Scott-Jones (1985) note that "this decline occurred during a period of time when the number of faculty positions increased by more than 5,000 and the number of blacks receiving Ph.D.s increased by more than 200" (p. 69). Sandoval (1983) reports that the latest national report (in 1979) estimated that the total percentage of black faculty was 4.4, with the percentage of black faculty at predominantly white institutions being much lower. Recent estimates suggest the figure for predominantly white campuses is 1-2 percent (Mackey-Smith, 1984).

With the exception of Asian-Americans, the representation of faculty from other ethnic groups is even lower on most campuses. For example, the number of American Indians/Alaskan Natives employed full time in 1983 was increased by only 22 people from 1981, while the number of Hispanics increased by about 450 individuals (Vetter and Babco, 1987; see also Aguirre, 1985). Moreover, the representation of women among these groups is small. For example, black women compose only 2 percent of all faculty members and are 7 percent of female faculty generally (Harvey and Scott-Jones, 1985).

These are dismal data to report for a decade and more of effort. Lack of significant change has been attributed to numerous factors, including a slower labor market for faculty in the 1970s and the lack of qualified women and minorities in certain fields, such as business and engineering, that were experiencing growth. If that has been the case, then the period of the late 1980s to mid 1990s will perhaps show considerable improvement. National projections suggest there will be a large number of retirements and an increasingly diverse pipeline of candidates for many fields. But few veterans of affirmative action feel complacent; much should be done besides gearing up for busier hiring activity. The role institutional research can and does play in assisting these efforts is crucial to their success.

Establishment of Internal Affirmative Action Targets

To improve the record on affirmative action, it may be helpful to examine the overall system of faculty careers. (See also the discussion of career phases in Chapter Two.) Figure 1 shows how women and men are recruited, selected, moved into the probationary period, passed through the tenure phase, and then moved into the ranks of senior faculty as associate and full professors. The career course terminates with retirement. Three factors turn this diagram into a dynamic process; namely, the entry of faculty into the process, their movement through it, and their departure from it. By understanding in detail what is occurring in each phase, trouble spots can be identified and assistance can be targeted more appropriately. The model has essentially three phases: the hiring phase, the probationary or pretenure period, and the permanent phase.

Phase 1: Hiring. The first phase of the process includes the four steps that lead to hiring new faculty: identifying and developing the pool of potential candidates, conducting a search, making the offer and finally,

Figure 1. Model of Faculty Hiring and Retention

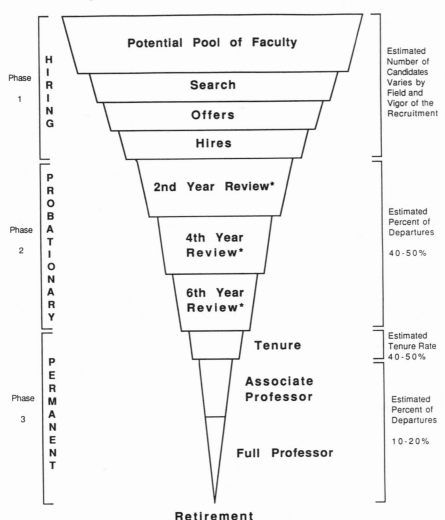

* Many institutions conduct reviews in the first, third, fifth, and sixth years.

formalizing the hiring with a contract. During the first two steps, the effort is on identifying candidates and encouraging them to be considered in the search. These are critical steps for increasing the number of women and minorities; hence, those responsible for affirmative action expend considerable effort here in establishing the pool and in attempting to ensure that a wide net is cast to garner a large number of diverse candidates. Search committees that go about their business at this stage in a perfunctory manner by relying solely on customary networks and colleagues will predispose the outcome by limiting the number and quality of candidates who can be considered in all subsequent stages (Hanna, 1988). It is in the interest of an institution to be in control of the process and to be in the position to select from the richest pool of talent possible. Thus, the first checkpoint in a high-quality affirmative action process is to review the size and diversity of the pool of candidates. When an institution is conducting relatively few searches, this is not difficult; but when many are occurring simultaneously, it is more challenging.

Once the search has identified acceptable candidates, the institution should ensure its chances of success for getting the candidates it wants. If the institution wants to increase the likelihood that faculty from under-represented groups are selected, it needs to ensure that its offers to them are attractive so that desirable candidates do not drop out. Potential threats to these objectives occur when: (1) qualified women and minority candidates are identified in the search but do not end up receiving an offer; (2) offers are not really competitive or attractive; and (3) follow-up to the offer is inadequate to successfully entice the candidate to sign a contract.

Research suggests that problems can occur at any of these points. For example, one study shows that while search committees may identify satisfactory women candidates, the hiring administrators may not make offers to them (Fulton, 1983). The process of monitoring searches, which is usually conducted by the affirmative action office, enhances the institution's effectiveness in making offers. Directives from the president and provost that hold administrators accountable for meeting their targets are also helpful if truly enforced (Menges and Exum, 1983). Annual information on an institution's hiring ratio by department is one indicator that an office of institutional research, in conjunction with the affirmative action office, can provide to monitor progress and reinforce executive directives.

Phase 2: Probationary Period. The next important phase of the hiring and retention model is the probationary or pretenure period. Many colleges and universities break this phase into steps by mandating annual or biennial reviews of candidates prior to tenure. While such regular performance reviews are considered good practice, evidence from some institutions suggests that this part of the process needs greater attention.

Attrition during these years appears to be quite high. Some estimates suggest it is as high as 40 percent for males and 60 percent for females prior to the tenure year (Strategic Study Group on the Status of Women, 1986–88).

Some attrition during these years is to be expected as young faculty test, often for the first time, whether they like and are successful at being full-fledged faculty members. Moreover, annual or biennial formal reviews are points at which an institution can make assessments concerning the ability and fit of the faculty member with its standards and objectives. Nevertheless, if an institution is interested in increasing the number of women or minorities on its faculty, it must strive to retain a larger group of its recruits up to and through the tenure process. What are the problems in attaining this goal?

First, attrition during the pretenure years is often not identified as a problem. So much attention is focused on hiring and on tenure outcomes that what occurs in between is overlooked. Second, a high attrition rate (perhaps 50–60 percent) in the pretenure years suggests that recruitment and hiring are off target. Faculty may be recruited who are not suited to the job or the institution. In this case, the hiring process should be reviewed. However, it is also possible that other problems during the pretenure years stimulate early departures.

Exit interviews with minority and women faculty suggest that such factors as academic climate, professional isolation, and a "hidden workload" of advising, counseling, and committee assignments are primary factors in bringing about their departures. These matters rather than formal negative assessments of their work appear to be playing a major role in most of these decisions to leave prior to the tenure year (Strategic Study Group, 1986–88; see also Clark and Corcoran, 1986; Laury, 1988).

We are not suggesting that an institution does not have the right or the obligation to make professional assessments during the probationary period. But we are concerned with whether institutions are aware of the above problems and their role in the loss of women and minorities prior to the tenure decision. If not, and if the institution's academic officers wish to retain a greater share of their junior faculty recruits, then several issues should be considered.

First, academic gatekeepers must openly acknowledge and discuss their role in sustaining faculty through the pretenure period. Some department heads and senior faculty operate under a Darwinian philosophy that the best probationary faculty will survive no matter what occurs in these early years. These individuals appear to believe they have only limited responsibility to sustain young faculty through this period. In their view, much can be said for a sink-or-swim approach. Perhaps this is true if plenty of desirable new recruits are available, if plenty of time and money can be expended in recruiting them, and if the ones who sink are indeed the undesirables. However, each of these premises is questionable. High-quality women and minority faculty are not plentiful in many fields; resources are tight at most institutions; and perhaps equally important, the probationary faculty often go to competitive institutions on what they perceive to be better terms.

To combat attrition in the pretenure years, institutions need to take a more corporate approach and invest in the success of junior faculty. Department heads and senior faculty should be encouraged to adopt the attitude that their search for a new faculty member has produced a potentially successful (that is, "tenurable") person. Henceforth, it is expected that serious and sustained efforts will be made to guide that candidate's development during the probationary years (see Chapter Two).

Second, the institution should review and sharpen the information system surrounding tenure. Accurate communication about tenure requirements and expectations for candidates in repeated, multiple formats is desirable. Many untenured faculty have the impression that the process is ambiguous, arbitrary, and even malicious. This must be combated in positive ways. Regular and frequent career conversations in addition to the biennial formal performance evaluations for probationary faculty seem especially needed. Another approach would be to institute a faculty mentor program by assigning senior faculty to work with junior faculty members. A number of institutions already do this or are considering it (Sandler and Hall, 1986). Finally, accurate information about the attrition rate during the pretenure years through cohort studies or other means is needed by department heads, deans, and central administrators and should be shared with faculty.

In any case, the greatest mistake a department head and dean can make with probationary faculty is to assume that young faculty know what is expected of them and how to go about it. The mistake can be immeasurably compounded if it is accompanied by the attitude that faculty who do not know what is expected of them are not wanted anyway. This is prejudicial on its face and represents the worst sort of personnel practice.

Women and minorities are not alone in needing repeated, clear-cut information on tenure requirements, procedures, and processes. Department heads and deans must be scrupulous in carrying out their responsibility to communicate directly and thoroughly to all probationary faculty on tenure matters. If they do not believe it is their responsibility, then they must be told so. Academic officers as well as affirmative action officers can prepare materials and delivery methods for these communications. Institutional research personnel can back these procedures with information on attrition to suggest where junior faculty may be encountering greater difficulties.

Tenure must never be treated as a contest in which some are inherently advantaged while others are not (Clark and Corcoran, 1986). Rather it is preferable to think of tenure as a key personnel decision in which much is invested and much is expected by both the institution and the candidate. Turning around a deeply rooted sink-or-swim approach to one that invests in people may be the single most important goal that provosts, deans, and department heads can pursue, especially in disciplines competing for faculty talent. Some institutions are already determined to make their mark as being especially hospitable to women and minorities. They are doing so with the understanding that they will be ahead of many others in the event of a significantly tighter marketplace.

Phase 3: Permanent Status. Upon securing tenure, two basic steps remain for the last phase of the career model: achieving associate- and, finally, full-professor rank. (A third step, preretirement, is emerging, but for our purposes is not explored.) While job mobility is a possibility in most academic careers, institutions need to be concerned with what they can do to retain as many of their permanent women and minority faculty as possible. Otherwise, the senior ranks can become depleted, and replacements are expensive when the costs of a search, the person's move, and increased salary are taken into account.

Most colleges and universities have only a small percentage of senior-level minorities and women. These persons provide many valuable services as scholars, leaders, role models, and mentors to other faculty as well as students. Some reduction in their numbers due to job mobility and retirement is to be expected. However, if departures exceed the normal, small percentages or are the result of systematically negative reasons, there is cause for concern, especially if other women and minorities are not moving through the tenure process in goodly numbers.

The usual reasons for the departures of senior women and minorities are a combination of push and pull factors. They are pulled by excellent job opportunities, often based on vigorous recruitment by other institutions, and are aided by the perception that a better challenge is available to them elsewhere. Push factors usually refer to negative circumstances at the departmental or college level. Many mention salary as a central issue as well as lack of appreciation and recognition for their contributions. Some do not hesitate to say, however, that they view the overall climate for women and minorities as less than satisfactory and do not see positive change occurring.

Clearly many institutions will be competing fiercely for the talented minorities and women who are available or who can be persuaded to move. Among these competing institutions, some will be able to match if not exceed current salaries. However, though it is usually a necessary condition, salary is normally insufficient for a successful "raid"; other factors also weigh heavily. According to many women and minority scholars, these include a positive attitude toward them on campus and generous conditions for work (Strategic Study Group, 1986–88).

Surprisingly, a number of senior faculty who left their institutions have noted that they were not encouraged to stay. Few reported receiving counteroffers or having serious conversations with department heads or deans about their concerns (Harvey and Scott-Jones, 1985). Indeed, many had the general sense that their college or university cared little about their leaving.

Based on such common, though anecdotal, accounts, it seems clear that colleges and universities need to develop better tracking mechanisms for faculty departures. Confusion often exists between central records offices, affirmative action offices, and individual deans' offices. Having accurate baseline information through a centralized reporting system that is computerized for easy access and manipulation is greatly needed. Exit interviews can provide much helpful information if done well. At minimum a brief, voluntary departure survey can be used, but the neutrality of the unit gathering the data is an important consideration. A few institutions already have such procedures in place; others will add them as the need to understand their own faculty dynamics increases. This is an area in which academic affairs and institutional research can work closely together.

Despite their senior status and the relatively long time they have spent in their academic communities, many present and former senior women and minorities speak of experiences similar to those of junior women and minorities—that is, a negative climate, professional isolation, and the pressures of hidden workloads (Strategic Study Group, 1986–88; Sandler and Hall, 1986). Some have recently perceived a more positive recognition of senior women and minorities, a greater willingness to appoint them to positions of power as well as service, and a more public acknowledgment of their contributions. It remains to be seen whether the perceived changes persist. One woman summarized the sentiments of many when she said, "The system does work, and it has protections built in, but you have to be willing to fight and to risk your career in order to succeed. . . . I for one think that it is too high and too unfair a price for women to have to pay. We can do better" (personal communication). Many minority faculty would echo her sentiments. What then can be done to improve the record of affirmative action, and how can institutional research be helpful?

Ways and Means of Improving the Record

The recommendations that follow are derived from the thoughts and experiences of numerous individuals and institutions. To our knowledge, however, no single institution has adopted all or even most of them. Rather, most institutions try to implement some things, but few have made a systematic, thorough review of their situation relative to women and minorities and devised a similarly thorough approach. There are exceptions such as the University of California (Justus, Freitag, and Parker, 1987), the University of Minnesota (Spector, 1988), the University of New Hampshire (Graulich, no date), and the University of Wisconsin (Erdman, 1981) to name a few of the larger institutions (see also Hyer, 1985). Others have made exemplary efforts in certain aspects of affirmative action, such as assistance for dual-career couples or minority faculty. They all deserve better notice. Invariably the arguments that undergird each of these institutional efforts are built on accurate, powerful institutional information.

A particularly good example of the effective use of institutional research information and staff is present in the reports of the Strategic Study Group on the Status of Women of The Pennsylvania State University (1986-88). Here institutional information was used throughout the study process, and research staff were invaluable in both assembling existing data and developing new information. Indeed, the experience of both authors in the work of that study group has guided the preparation of this chapter and the development of the recommendations presented below.

While this final section deals with improvements that can be made once an individual has chosen to enter a faculty career, it is worth mentioning that colleges and universities can do much to encourage women and minorities to pursue graduate education and academic careers. Because of the large numbers of faculty who will retire in the next ten to fifteen years, a tremendous opportunity exists to improve the representation of women and minorities on the faculty. The development of potential faculty should begin early by exposing high school students to faculty women and minorities and by offering career exploration opportunities on campus. Undergraduate students should receive encouragement through opportunities to work closely with faculty on research projects and by being apprised of fellowships and assistantships for further study. At the graduate level, women and minority students need opportunities to work closely with their counterparts through mentor relationships and through research and teaching. They need to be encouraged to consider academic careers and to see these faculty as prestigious and rewarded members of their institutions (Michigan Association of Governing Boards, 1988; Sandler and Hall, 1986).

The suggestions that follow are organized around the series of problems described above and build upon the recommendations embedded in the original concept of affirmative action shaped nearly two decades ago.

To enhance the academic climate for women and minorities:

1. Urge the president and chief academic officer of the institution to express in public statements their commitment to increasing the number and participation of women and minorities on the faculty. They must

continue to demonstrate their commitment through their willingness to appoint women and minorities and through their watchfulness over the various hiring, tenure, and retention policies and practices. They must not hesitate to discipline individuals and units who engage in activities such as sexual harassment that serve to discourage or discriminate against the full participation of women and minorities.

2. Initiate a series of workshops on gender and racial bias for those in the tenure and promotion process. These workshops could address issues like perceptual bias, the treatment of women and minority faculty in informal professional interactions, the denigration of research on women or ethnic groups or research in areas dominated by women or minorities, and the problems of hidden workload.

3. Urge appropriate faculty governance units to address the creation of an academic climate that welcomes and supports people of diverse backgrounds and with diverse academic interests. The richness of diversity is to be stressed rather than the comfort of homogeneity.

4. Review every campus committee to ensure that women and minorities are members whenever possible. While being mindful of not over-burdening people with committee assignments, the institution should make it clear that their inclusion is essential and appreciated.

5. Maintain accurate lists of women and minorities by discipline and rank as a ready resource when internal appointments are being made.

6. Take steps to increase the number of women and minorities appointed as department heads and other administrative officers without, however, jeopardizing their chances to achieve full-professor rank.

To reduce professional isolation of women:

1. Provide new-faculty orientation programs that address issues of professional isolation and provide information regarding the networks of women and minority scholars.

2. Provide funds for the development of programs that will help women and minority faculty to connect with peers and senior scholars who work in their areas of interest both within the institution and at other places. This may require providing summer stipends or leaves of absence or opportunities for senior scholars to spend short periods of time as scholars-in-residence.

3. Encourage various academic units to develop programs that pair senior faculty as mentors with junior faculty to guide and encourage their work in research, teaching, and service. Reward the efforts of senior faculty who participate. Such efforts are particularly important in areas such as the sciences and engineering, where women or minorities are few in number, but all units should be encouraged.

To reduce the stress of the hidden workload:

1. Encourage faculty to document fully the work they do as advisers

to students and student groups and the extent of their service on committees. Ensure that these will be taken into account along with teaching and research at all levels of the tenure and promotion process.

2. Provide assistance to dual-career couples for whom at least one spouse is being considered for or is seeking employment in the institution. Assist department heads and deans in working with potential faculty members when a spouse's employment is a concern. Convey a positive attitude toward dual-career couples by making available various types of employment, housing, and child-care information. Extend similar assistance to faculty who are single or who have other types of family obligations (for example, an elderly dependent).

3. Review, clarify, and disseminate the institution's policy on maternity leave. Insure that adoptive parents are included. Consider creating a policy to permit probationary faculty to be granted up to one extra year of tenure eligibility after the birth or adoption of a child.

4. Undertake a needs assessment study of child care within the community in preparation for planned initiatives in this area.

To enhance hiring women and minority faculty:

1. Create an "opportunity fund" to provide money for hiring outstanding senior women and minority faculty who are identified but for whom no vacancy is currently available; or for supplementing salaries to be competitive with other institutions; or for initiating special outreach and recruitment efforts.

2. Strongly encourage heads of academic units to appoint minorities and women as chairs of search committees, to include at least one woman member on every search committee for a full- or associate-professor position, and to make every effort to include women and minorities on all faculty search committees.

3. Insist on active search and recruitment of women and minority candidates by contacting appropriate publications and organizations, by insuring that every position advertisement explicitly encourages women and minorities to apply, and by using vitae banks whenever possible. Review the advertisements recently published by each unit.

4. Hold appointing administrators accountable for meeting their affirmative action targets. Reward departments that perform well.

5. Gather information on women and minority candidates who were not successfully recruited and conduct follow-up interviews with such persons concerning the reasons they did not choose to come to the institution.

To enhance retention of women and minority faculty:

1. Improve the information on departure and retention rates at all phases of the academic career system. Routinely conduct interviews of

faculty members who are about to leave the institution or devise and administer an exit questionnaire.

2. Charge department heads and deans with providing accurate, written guidelines to probationary faculty on a regular basis concerning the development of all aspects of their faculty careers. While not lessening the rigors of the tenure decision and the evaluations leading up to it, hold department heads accountable for encouraging and supporting women and minority probationary faculty. Give recognition and reward to those department heads who develop a record for recruiting and retaining women and minority faculty in their units.

3. Review and sharpen the information system surrounding tenure. Devise multiple ways of delivering information on tenure procedures, on building a dossier, on fulfilling and documenting multiple responsibilities, and on rights of appeal, so that the information reaches every probationary faculty member in an appropriate and timely way. The concerns of women and minority faculty should receive special attention.

4. Ensure that tenure track faculty receive first priority in setting up laboratories and other essential work facilities. Consider granting extra time to those who experience uncontrollable delays.

5. Encourage all promotion and tenure committees to discuss their standards for research, teaching, and service each year before beginning their work, and then to review them at the conclusion. Encourage committee members to participate in a workshop targeted at sensitizing them to the potential for gender and racial bias in the evaluation of faculty work and recommendations.

To encourage progress:

1. Establish a formal procedure to monitor the progress on these initiatives.

2. Provide a report to the community every twelve to fifteen months.

Conclusion

The experiences since the first legislation concerning affirmative action and equity in 1972 have shown that legislation alone cannot achieve the desired outcomes. Every institution, its leaders, faculty, students, and staff, must be knowledgeable about and committed to the principles and practices that undergird our legal commitment. Moreover, each institution, through the efforts of its faculty and staff, must devise a system that will best suit its needs, its history, its clientele, and its future. This system will not occur by accident. It will take the coordinated effort of many individuals, who are aided and supported by accurate information and understanding as much as by the simple willingness to bring about change on behalf of women and minorities. The knowledge and expertise housed in offices of institutional research are indispensable to devising a workable and farsighted system. Skilled and energetic participation by professionals in the institution's efforts toward increasing equity among faculty, staff, and students is essential. Those of us who have worked closely with such professionals in affirmative action know what a significant difference their efforts can make. Surely the dignified and vital future of our institutions is the ultimate beneficiary of these efforts.

References

Aguirre, A., Jr. "Chicano Faculty at Postsecondary Educational Institutions in the Southwest." *Journal of Educational Equity and Leadership*, 1985, 5 (2), 133–144.

Bowen, H. R., and Schuster, J. H. *American Professors: A National Resource Imperiled*. New York: Oxford University Press, 1986.

Carnegie Commission on Higher Education. *Opportunities for Women*. Carnegie Commission Report. New York: McGraw-Hill, 1973.

Carnegie Commission on Higher Education. *Making Affirmative Action Work*. San Francisco: Jossey-Bass, 1975.

Clark, S. M., and Corcoran, M. "Perspectives on the Professional Socialization of Women Faculty: A Case of Accumulative Disadvantages?" *Journal of Higher Education*, 1986, 57 (1), 20–43.

Erdman, J. M. "A Blueprint for Achievement of Educational Equality in the Eighties." A Report of the Regent's Task Force on the Status of Women. Madison: University of Wisconsin, April 1981.

Etaugh, C. "Women Faculty and Administrators in Higher Education: Changes in Their Status Since 1972." *Journal of the National Association of Women Deans, Administrators and Counselors*, 1984, 48 (1), 21–25.

Finkelstein, M. J. "The Status of Academic Women: An Assessment of Five Competing Explanations." *Review of Higher Education*, 1984, 7, 119–141.

Fulton, B. F. "Access for Minorities and Women to Administrative Leadership Positions: Influence of the Search Committee." *Journal of the National Association of Women Deans, Administrators and Counselors*, 1983, 47 (1), 3–7.

Gappa, J., and Uehling, B. S. *Women in Academe: Steps to Greater Equality*. ASHE-ERIC Higher Education Research Report, no. 1. Washington, D.C.: American Association for Higher Education, 1979.

Graulich, M. (ed.). *Closing the Revolving Door: The Retention of Women in Higher Education*. President's Commission on the Status of Women. Manchester: University of New Hampshire, n.d.

Hanna, C. "The Organizational Context for Affirmative Action for Women Faculty." *Journal of Higher Education*, 1988, 59 (4), 390–411.

Harvey, W. B., and Scott-Jones, D. "We Can't Find Any: The Elusiveness of Black Faculty Members in American Higher Education." *Issues in Education*, 1985, 3 (1), 68–76.

Hendrickson, R. M. and Lee, B. A. *Academic Employment and Retrenchment: Judicial Review and Administrative Action*. ASHE-ERIC Higher Education Research Report, no. 8. Washington, D.C.: Association for the Study of Higher Education, 1983.

Hyer, P. B. "Affirmative Action for Women Faculty: Case Studies of Three Successful Institutions." *Journal of Higher Education*, 1985, 56 (3), 282–299.

Justus, J. B., Freitag, S. B., and Parker, L. L. *The University of California in the Twenty-First Century: Successful Approaches to Faculty Diversity.* Berkeley: University of California, 1987.

Keller, G. "The New Management Revolution in Higher Education." *AAHE Bulletin,* 1982, *35* (2), 3–5.

Koch, J. V. "Salary Equity Issues in Higher Education: Where Do We Stand?" *AAHE Bulletin,* 1982, *35* (2), 7–14.

LaNoue, G. R., and Lee, B. A. *Academics in Court: Consequences of Faculty Discrimination Litigation.* Ann Arbor: University of Michigan Press, 1987.

Laury, M. M. "Contributing Factors in Career Advancement of Black Faculty Members at Traditionally White Institutions." Unpublished doctoral dissertation, Division of Education Policy Studies, The Pennsylvania State University, 1988.

Lester, R. A. *Antibias Regulation of Universities.* Report for the Carnegie Commission on Higher Education. New York: McGraw-Hill, 1974.

Lindgren, J. R., Ota, P., Zirkel, P., and Gieson, N. V. *Sex Discrimination Law in Higher Education: The Lesson of the Past Decade.* ASHE-ERIC Higher Education Research Report, no. 4. Washington. D.C.: Association for the Study of Higher Education, 1984.

Mackey-Smith, A. "Large Shortage of Black Professors in Higher Education Grows Worse." *The Wall Street Journal,* June 12, 1984, p. 37.

McMillen, L. "Women Professors Pressing to Close Salary Gap." *Chronicle of Higher Education,* 1987, *33* (44), 1.

Menges, R. J., and Exum, W. H. "Barriers to the Progress of Women and Minority Faculty." *Journal of Higher Education,* 1983, *54* (2), 123–144.

Michigan Association of Governing Boards. *Report on the Status of Women Faculty in Michigan Public Universities.* Lansing: Michigan Association of Governing Boards, October 1988.

Reed, R. J. "Affirmative Action in Higher Education: Is It Necessary?" *Journal of Negro Education,* 1983, *52* (3), 332–349.

Sandler, B. R., and Hall, R. *The Campus Climate Revisited: Chilly for Women, Faculty, Administration, and Graduate Students.* Project on the Status of Women. Washington, D.C.: American Association of Colleges, 1986.

Sandoval, P. *Minorities in Higher Education.* Washington, D.C.: American Council on Education, 1983.

Spector, J. D. "The Minnesota Plan II." *Internal Report.* Minneapolis: University of Minnesota, 1988.

Strategic Study Group on the Status of Women. *Report to the President and the Commission for Women.* Recommendation packages nos. 1–5 and Final Report. University Park: Office of Planning and Analysis, Pennsylvania State University, 1986–88.

Vetter, B., and Babco, E. L. *Professional Women and Minorities: A Manpower Data Resource Service.* Washington D.C.: Scientific Manpower Commission, 1987.

Widnall, S. E. "AAAS Presidential Lecture: Voices from the Pipeline." *Science,* September 30, 1988, *241,* 1740–1745.

Kathryn M. Moore is professor of education policy and leadership in the Department of Educational Administration at Michigan State University.

Michael P. Johnson is associate professor of sociology at The Pennsylvania State University.

Managing faculty resources effectively requires an
understanding of the unique organizational characteristics
of colleges and universities. Within this distinctive setting,
a variety of methodological tools exist to monitor resource
needs and applications.

Balancing Faculty Resources and Institutional Needs

Karen D. Byers, Cynthia A. Linhart, Michael J. Dooris

The key to success for colleges and universities rests principally with their ability to manage resources well, and their most important resource is their faculties. Success requires balancing the institution's goals and needs with the personal and professional needs of individual faculty members. The distinctive organizational configuration of academic institutions and the special character of the faculty and what they do present higher education with unusual management challenges.

This chapter considers how institutions can balance faculty resources and institutional needs. We begin by pointing out characteristics that distinguish management in the academy from management in other settings. We also discuss the special nature of faculty members as professionals and the roles of academic managers in this unique setting. The chapter then provides examples of the methodologies, tools, and techniques institutional researchers can employ to assist academic managers in their decision making.

Management in the College and University Setting

Academia is an enterprise devoted to acquiring, creating, using, and disseminating knowledge. The work of the faculty sustains the basic

G. G. Lozier and M. J. Dooris (eds.). *Managing Faculty Resources.*
New Directions for Institutional Research, no. 63. San Francisco: Jossey-Bass, Fall 1989.

mission of the institution, and it is this work with which academic management is concerned. To understand academic management, we have to consider the unique organization of the college or university.

Academic Institutions as Organizations. Management strategies successful in corporate settings typically have not worked well in higher education, in large part because the organizational dynamics of colleges and universities differ markedly from the business environment. Corson (1975) has observed that "the character of organizations—the kind of environment they provide for their members—flows from the purpose for which they exist and the nature of the activities they carry on" (p. 161). A number of key differences between colleges and universities and other organizations can be cited.

1. The purpose of a college or university, as described in its mission, is as much to facilitate a process as it is to generate a product. An ongoing set of activities in this setting leads to an ongoing set of outcomes.

2. A college or university has no readily apparent "bottom line" against which to measure success. Indeed, it may receive conflicting signals; for example, applications at a college are down this year, but three of last year's graduates received Fulbright fellowships. Fiscal health is one measure, applications another, faculty publications yet a third, and so on.

3. Not only is it difficult to define a full set of measures that portray the activities and achievements of the institution, but many individuals and offices are responsible for defining and collecting data. Typically, academic managers operate in a local sphere with incomplete or inconsistent information and under varying degrees of uncertainty.

4. Governance, an especially distinctive feature of academic institutions, has an enormous impact on academic management. Trustees have legal authority for overseeing the institution, but decision making often falls to faculty, administrators, the president, and the board. Colleges and universities have been variously characterized by analysts as bureaucratic, collegial, anarchic, loosely coupled, and political (Austin and Gamson, 1983) and more recently as cybernetic (Birnbaum, 1988).

5. The institution consists of a wide variety of departments and subunits, each with its own distinctive mission and culture. Faculty in each of these subunits exhibit different attitudes, values, and personal characteristics (Bowen and Schuster, 1986).

Within this organizational context, "the faculty . . . tend to think of themselves as being the university" (Besse, 1973, p. 109). Who are the faculty and what are faculty resources? These two crucial questions must be addressed if we are to understand the management of faculty.

Faculty as Resources. Faculty resources can be defined as the knowledge, talent, intellect, skills, experience, and creativity that faculty members individually and collectively bring to an institution. The faculty teach students, conduct research, publish papers, develop new products, treat patients, and determine the educational program. They are professionals engaged in the business of learning and can be distinguished from their professional counterparts in other fields by at least four characteristics.

1. While the predominant and most visible activity of faculty members is teaching, few are trained to teach. As graduate students, their primary activity was research and scholarship (Brookes and German, 1983). More than any other group of professionals, they can be characterized as scholars, as seekers of new knowledge—in short, as professional learners.

2. Faculty members have no unifying professional identity. Instead, their professional identity is a function of their academic discipline, since their training and experience are with a specific body of knowledge (Austin and Gamson, 1983). Not only is the concept of a homogeneous profession confounded by disciplinary subcultures (Kuh and Whitt, 1988), but these subcultures also influence differences in teaching and research responsibilities. For example, a music professor may teach piano one-on-one, while an accounting professor may teach several large lecture courses. A microbiologist may have access to a wide variety of external funds for research, while a philosophy or English professor typically has to rely on institutional funds to travel to a distant library.

3. No single element of what faculty members do distinguishes them from other professionals (Brookes and German, 1983) except that they are employed only by colleges and universities. People in elementary schools and corporations also teach; researchers in industrial and federal laboratories make groundbreaking discoveries; essayists and independent intellectuals stretch the boundaries of our understanding of events and issues; but while a doctor or lawyer is always a doctor or lawyer, regardless of the organization in which he or she works, a professor is only a professor when employed by academic institution. Thus, the academic professional is exceptionally dependent upon a specific institutional setting to carry out a career (Shulman, 1979; Austin and Gamson, 1983).

4. No profession outside of the field of education offers tenure.
The distinctive nature of academic institutions and the unique characteristics of faculty members have a significant impact on academic management and on how faculty resources are deployed by the institution.

The Role of the Academic Manager. The task of academic managers is to create an environment that will balance the autonomy and individuality of the faculty members with the constraints and accountabilities of the department or college. In addition, this balance must be consistent with the expectations set by institutional and state boards, federal and state legislatures, and other external constituencies.

Academic management entails making decisions and taking actions in a setting of collegiality and peer relationships. We can define academic management as a process by which decisions pertaining to the *allocation* of resources (hiring, staffing, terminating), the *utilization* of resources (deployment and promotion), and the *projection* of future resources needs are made and carried out (Gonyea, 1981). The academic managers themselves are typically members of the faculty who hold the titles of president, vice president for academic affairs (or provost), dean, or department chair. (The academic manager can also be a faculty member who takes on a particular managerial role, such as chair of a search or curriculum review committee, and whose actions in that role may impact the institution's allocation and utilization of resources. Such temporary roles are not included in this discussion.)

A major responsibility of the academic manager is to deliver and monitor institutional resources so that students are educated and graduated, research and scholarship is conducted, and public service is provided. As we consider the methodologies and tools available to managers, we must be mindful of the uniqueness of the faculty as human resources and the distinctiveness of the collegiate settings in which they work.

Tools and Techniques for Managing Faculty Resources

Despite the many aspects of colleges and universities that make managing faculty different from human resource management in other employment settings, the college or university, like other service organizations, government bureaus, and certain corporate settings, is a labor-intensive enterprise. As Corson (1973) notes, the institution "is dependent on the caliber, the effectiveness, and the zeal of the human resources it assembles" (p. 163).

In the remaining sections, we examine methodologies by which institutional researchers can support academic managers as they strive to realize the maximum potential of their college or university's faculty resources. While recognizing that some methodological limitations (such as unresolved problems of definition and measurement) are inherent in any technique dealing with faculty allocation, we suggest a number of techniques institutional researchers may find useful for analyzing faculty allocation. In each case, specific approaches are reviewed only briefly, with suggestions for where the interested reader can find more-detailed information.

Methodological Limitations

A variety of methodologies can be and have been adapted to faculty allocation analysis. In the attempt to develop and apply tools for resource management decisions, institutional researchers have faced at least six generic problems.

1. Analytical techniques have not evolved systematically. In higher education (as in other fields) the "hot buttons" change over time; we are not necessarily methodical as we invent, refine, discard, and combine conceptual frameworks or analytical tools.

2. The sophistication of institutional data systems has powerfully influenced the extent to which various methodologies have been adopted. Institutional research practice has probably depended as much on data-processing capabilities as on institutional needs or methodological considerations.

3. Institutional data systems are created primarily to manage administrative processes such as payroll and registration. They have not typically been designed (and may not have the requisite data elements) to support faculty flow models, workload studies, and the like.

4. Because different disciplines (for example, accounting versus English) have different needs, cross-department comparability is a serious constraint for any faculty workload or productivity measure.

5. A number of potentially powerful statistical methods are not widely applied, perhaps because the hows and whys of their use are not always clearly presented.

6. Perhaps most fundamentally, no analytical methodologies have completely solved root definitional and measurement problems. What is faculty workload? How can it be validly and reliably measured? How should activities that produce multiple outcomes be addressed? How should we determine the number of faculty lines needed to achieve particular outcomes?

Designing Faculty Workload Studies

In theory the concept of faculty workload incorporates teaching, research, service to the community and the discipline, institutional governance, and professional development. Blackburn (1974) provides excellent insight into the complex, overlapping character of these activities and the measurement problems they imply. In practice, the results of studies of faculty workload are used by decision makers in collective bargaining, development of grant proposals, cost studies, equity analyses, budgeting, lawmaking, litigation, and in public relations activities (Yucker, 1984). The design of the workload study therefore depends both on conceptual dimensions and on the pragmatic needs and interests of academic managers who will use the information.

With this balance in mind, a few considerations hold regardless of how a particular study is designed. The purpose of the study should be clearly stated. This helps define the data to be collected and garners cooperation and support for the study. Researchers must be clear about whether, and why, the study is to be either normative and specific to a point in time or evaluative and longitudinal. The unit of analysis should be some collective grouping such as a department or school; from a policy-making perspective, little justification exists for studies that focus on individual faculty members. In addition, managers and researchers must be cautious about making comparisons among departments within a single campus. Fundamental differences, for example, may lie in the pedagogical or research needs and problems faced by different departments. Finally, study design should be sensitive to factors that may account for apparent differences in productivity, such as team teaching versus sole responsibility and the availability of graduate assistants or multiple course sections versus unique preparations. (Here the use of weighting schemes such as those suggested by Shull, 1984, may be helpful.)

Measuring Faculty Workload

Institutional researchers studying faculty workload and utilization typically choose from one or two basic approaches. The first relies on existing institutional data bases; the second uses faculty self-reports.

Studies of faculty workload based on institutionally available data typically employ variables such as:

- *Faculty credit hours,* the number of credit hours associated with a particular course.
- *Student credit hours (SCH),* the number of faculty credit hours multiplied by the number of students enrolled in a course.
- *SCH per full time-equivalent (FTE) faculty member,* a unit that requires the careful definition of FTE, including such dimensions as full versus part time, length of contract (for example, nine months versus twelve months), and responsibilities (for example, instruction, research, or administration).
- *Contact hours,* the number of class hours spent teaching a class. This value may differ significantly from faculty credit hours, particularly in laboratory, studio, and physical education courses.

Some studies have also considered student/faculty ratios as an indicator of faculty workload, although the validity of this indicator has been questioned. Most recent efforts to develop methodologies using institutional data have focused on the variables described above (Shulman, 1980; Bloom, 1982; Brown, 1984; Peat Marwick Main & Co., 1989).

A disadvantage of these indicators is that they are limited by the capabilities of data systems (such as course registration and transcript or payroll files) designed for other operations. Also, they tend to focus on instruction and to ignore or discount other components of faculty workload. However, measures based on institutionally available data are attractive because when carefully defined, they can facilitate inter-institutional data exchanges.

An alternative is the use of faculty self-reports of activity. Such faculty activity studies can transcend some of the limitations (especially the tendency to focus on instructional activities) inherent in the use of already available institutional data. However, validity may be questioned and inter-institutional comparability will be limited. Whether a given analysis should focus on actual hours spent or on relative effort expended should be addressed in the earliest stages of design (McLaughlin, Montgomery, Gravely, and Mahan, 1981). Choices must also be made about population definition, sampling procedures, and the use of questionnaires, interviews, diaries, work samples, and the like.

Certain institutions may be able to overcome some of the limitations of both centrally available data and faculty self-reports by developing internal measures based on a variety of information—not necessarily computerized—which can be accessed by institutional researchers. For example, in the late 1970s the University of Illinois at Chicago developed unit productivity ratios combining data on FTE students, publications, and external funding.

Because these measures can be based on units' prior experiences, departments that have historically had little external funding would not be penalized. For such units external funding would always have represented a relatively small share of their index; therefore, changes in a given unit's productivity ratio over time would reliably represent increases or decreases in productivity. Such indexes allow researchers and managers to make meaningful comparisons among disciplines about productivity changes over time.

In spite of fundamental practical difficulties in how we measure workload and productivity, a variety of methodological tools can be applied to the analysis of faculty resources. Three approaches are described below. Modeling techniques describe the relationship among resources, constraints, and desired outcomes and can be used to evaluate alternatives. Analytical techniques (for example, position control) link the setting of priorities and the allocation of faculty resources to planning and budgeting processes. Forecasting techniques allow projections of both the supply of and demand for faculty.

Modeling Techniques

In principle, the goals, requirements, constraints, and relationships of managing faculty resources can be modeled in a fairly straightforward manner. Essentially, the institution wishes to maximize faculty output (however measured) from the available resources. At the same time, the institution is subject to a set of constraints such as money, tenure policies, faculty turnover rates, limits on workload, and so on.

Wallhaus (1980) uses this basic framework, familiar to students of linear programming, to build a mathematical model for allocating resources to maximize benefits. As Wallhaus points out, this formulation is an appropriate point of departure for analyzing and making decisions about resource allocation, utilization, and planning. He offers a few examples of its application (see Walters, Mangold, and Haran, 1976; Schroeder, 1974; and Wallhaus, 1971).

Resource/Outcome Models. Decisions about the allocation of faculty resources are ultimately part of larger budgeting processes. A number of methodologies have focused on the relationship between resource allocation and outcomes—primarily from the institutional perspective as opposed, for example, to departmental or state perspectives (Montgomery, McLaughlin, and Mahan, 1981; Ramsey, Hardwick, and Ainsworth 1981; Brown, 1984).

The late 1960s and the 1970s saw the development of many computerized models, such as RRPM (Resource Requirements Prediction Model), CAMPUS (Comprehensive Analytical Models for Planning in University/College Systems), HELP/Plantran (Higher Education Long-Range Planning/Planning Translator), and SEARCH (System for Evaluating Alternative Resource Commitments in Higher Education). The models typically related faculty resources to instructional productivity and on that basis—and with limited user flexibility—suggested allocations to specific organizational units. (For a review of the experience of four hundred institutions with such models, see Plourde, 1976.) The EDUCOM Financial Planning Model (EFPM) gave modelers more flexibility to describe alternative resource and outcome relationships. The advent of personal computers has further encouraged institutional researchers to tailor specific resource-allocation tools.

Multi-Attribute Utility Models. Yet another approach to resource-allocation decisions uses what are known as multi-attribute utility models. A formal introduction to such models and their application in a variety of settings is provided by Keeney and Raiffa (1976).

In essence, multi-attribute utility modeling is a mathematical procedure by which alternatives are evaluated in terms of predetermined criteria. For example, an academic unit employing a multi-attribute utility model for faculty resource decisions would begin by defining such attributes as ethnic diversity, research and scholarship, a flat faculty age distribution, and an adequate mix of disciplinary specialties. It then is necessary to weight the importance of each attribute and to define a set of alternatives that can achieve the specified attributes. The mathematical model measures show how well the alternatives satisfy the objectives.

Multi-attribute utility modeling is not yet widely adopted in higher education, although its use in support of faculty personnel decisions has been described by McCartt (1986). A primary asset of the multi-attribute utility model is that it requires the resource manager to identify an established set of desirable attributes. Secondarily, as a mathematical model, it provides numerical results on which decisions can be based.

Analytical Techniques

Position Control. Position control is a technique employed by institutions and some states to manage the allocation of faculty resources. Under position control, the re-allocation of positions is not controlled at the unit (the department or school) to which lines are assigned. Instead, position allocations are monitored and evaluated at some higher level, such as the college, institution, or state. The priorities at that higher level thus become the basis for reassigning vacant lines. The goal of position control is to avoid both over- and understaffing and to broaden perspectives as to what constitutes the optimal utilization of resources.

The disadvantages of position control include the limitations on decentralized management and the ability of a unit to respond to changes in disciplinary directions, research emphases, and student demands. Another drawback is that administrative procedures necessary to monitor a position-control process, consider rejustification requests, and oversee re-allocation are time consuming.

Cost Studies. Both position control and resource/outcome models are tied to institutional budgeting processes. Complementing these approaches are cost studies, which consider not only the direct costs of faculty but also their indirect costs, such as graduate assistants, secretarial support, equipment, supplies, and travel. (For additional information on cost studies and models, see Gonyea, 1978.)

Forecasting Techniques

The responsibility to project a college or university's faculty resource needs typically focuses managers' attention on instructional activities. This emphasis primarily reflects the importance of instruction in all types of colleges and universities. It also shows that, although the various production functions developed around enrollment and student credit hour data have limitations, they have been accepted into the management environment as the most accessible operational definitions of faculty workload.

Initially the cadre of modeling tools introduced for the allocation of faculty resources (models such as RRPM, SEARCH, CAMPUS, and Plantran, based primarily on instructional demand) was also used to make projections. Institutional researchers and academic managers found that parameters could be manipulated to answer various "what if" questions. For example, what if the number of FTE majors declines in these four programs and increases in those two? What if we change curriculum requirements or teaching methods? Based on defined relationships between faculty resources and outcomes, analysts could begin to make projections, but their vision was limited to specific relationships described within the models and by the models' inordinate data needs. Such models focused on the impact of student demand on faculty resources and specifically attempted to identify where changes in faculty needs would occur (Campbell and Doan, 1983).

More recently, attention has been given to the supply side of faculty resources. How will the faculty look in terms of rank, tenure, gender, and age? What impact will changes in such characteristics have on the management of these resources—that is, on recruitment, affirmative action, promotion, and renewal? What impact will they have on the translation of the institution's mission into instruction, research, and service programs? The basic tool used to examine the supply side of faculty resources is the faculty flow model.

Markov Models. One approach well suited to the phenomenon of faculty flow is Markov modeling. Markov processes in general describe the movement of subjects through a system based on transition probabilities. Markov models allow one to project the behavior of faculty based on the characteristics of the faculty in place and on the probabilities of change. We can use past faculty flow patterns to develop probabilities (in the form of "transition matrices") that faculty will move from one category to another, as from employed to retired or from assistant professor to associate professor. These transition probabilities can then be applied to the current population of faculty to project trends of faculty change.

The mathematics of Markov models and their use in human resource planning has been thoroughly discussed by Hopkins (1974). In the academic setting, Spinney and McLaughlin (1979) describe the use of such models to assess alternate faculty-personnel policies, and Feldt (1986) examines how Markov models may be used to forecast work-force needs and plan reductions in force. The chapter on human resources planning in Hopkins and Massey (1981) presents both a conceptual framework and case applications for analyzing faculty appointment, promotion, and retirement policies. Such applications illustrate the adaptability and flexibility of Markov processes for predicting and analyzing dimensions of faculty flow, and for estimating the sensitivity of outcomes to adjustments in initial assumptions.

The major limitation of a Markov model applies to most predictive models—that is, the model is only as good as the assumptions built into it. For example, many of the predictions of a dramatic national enrollment decline a decade ago were based on Markov model studies. Because enrollments have actually increased, the models and the predictions have come under much criticism. However, the models' predictions would most likely have been correct in the absence of interventions. Largely as a result of studies using the Markov model, states and institutions initiated policies that increased the matriculation rate of high school graduates (especially women) and that promoted adult college attendance. These actions and others helped to deflect the impact of the decline in the number of traditional-age college students. Similarly, Markov model applications can assist in the identification of needed intervention strategies for faculty resources.

Other Forecasting Methods. In addition to Markov models, many other formal forecasting methodologies are available, but not always widely used, to predict faculty flows. Analysts may choose, for example, from a variety of time series approaches, which essentially extend previous observations into the future. Fundamentally different are techniques such as regression that predict the behavior of dependent variables based on structural relationships to independent variables. Yancey (1988) provides an exceptionally clear, readable, and up-to-date overview on the use of regression, path analysis, and LISREL; log-linear and logit models; and time series (in particular, Box-Jenkins) methods in institutional research settings.

Integrating Faculty Resource Analyses with Planning

Central to the idea that institutions must be well informed about their faculty resources is the notion of planning. Institutions expect their managers to be knowledgeable about resources and constraints, to identify desired outcomes, and to develop appropriate strategies to achieve those outcomes. Departmental goals will be shaped by those of the school or college, whose plans must be supportive of overall institutional objectives. Problems and opportunities must be placed within the context of overall institutional identity and mission. The existence of a plan permits the evaluation of whether, and to what extent, goals have been achieved.

If, as we believe, faculty time is the critical resource for colleges and universities, then an important element in planning and institutional decision making should be the efficient and effective use of faculty. Consistent with the broad notion of planning as preparing for and choosing among alternative futures, Gonyea (1981) sees four fundamental steps in optimizing the use of faculty resources: to describe current resource needs, to define constraints, to describe alternative futures, and to make choices. Gonyea suggests that academic managers must determine staffing needs, have some means for evaluating how well faculty time is utilized, and make decisions about the allocation of faculty resources that are consistent with the goals and mission of the institution. The institutional researcher, with the various tools available (including the methodologies suggested in this chapter) can help academic managers to more fully achieve these ends.

76

References

Austin, A. E., and Gamson, Z. F. *Academic Workplace: New Demands, Heightened Tensions.* ASHE-ERIC Higher Education Research Report, no. 10. Washington, D.C.: Association for the Study of Higher Education, 1983.

Besse, R. M. "A Comparison of the University with the Corporation." In J. A. Perkins (ed.), *The University as an Organization.* New York: McGraw-Hill, 1973.

Birnbaum, R. *How Colleges Work: The Cybernetics of Academic Organization and Leadership.* San Francisco: Jossey-Bass, 1988.

Blackburn, R. T. "The Meaning of Work in Academia." In J. I. Doi (ed.), *Assessing Faculty Effort.* New Directions for Institutional Research, no. 2. San Francisco: Jossey-Bass, 1974.

Bloom, A. M. "Differential Instructional Productivity Indices." Paper presented at the annual forum of the Association for Institutional Research, Denver, 1982.

Bowen, H. R., and Schuster, J. H. *American Professors: A National Resource Imperiled.* New York: Oxford University Press, 1986.

Brookes, M.C.T., and German, K. L. *Meeting the Challenges: Developing Faculty Careers.* ASHE-ERIC Higher Education Research Report, no. 3. Washington, D.C.: Association for the Study of Higher Education, 1983.

Brown, M. K. "In Search of a Fair Faculty Allocation Formula." Paper presented at the annual forum of the Association for Institutional Research, Fort Worth, Texas, 1984.

Campbell, W. E., and Doan, H. M. "Better Managerial Effectiveness Through Improved Planning and Budgeting in the Academic Area." Paper presented at the annual forum of the Association for Institutional Research, Toronto, 1983.

Corson, J. J. "Perspectives on the University Compared with Other Institutions." In J. A. Perkins (ed.), *The University as an Organization.* New York: McGraw-Hill, 1973.

Feldt, J. A. "Markov Models and Reductions in Work Force." In J. Rohrbaugh and A. T. McCartt (eds.), *Applying Decision Support Systems in Higher Education.* New Directions for Institutional Research, no. 49. San Francisco: Jossey-Bass, 1986.

Gonyea, M. A. (ed.). *Analyzing and Constructing Cost.* New Directions for Institutional Research, no. 17. San Francisco: Jossey-Bass, 1978.

Gonyea, M. A. "Determining Academic Staff Needs, Allocation, and Utilization." In P. Jedamus, M. W. Peterson, and Associates (eds.), *Improving Academic Management: A Handbook of Planning and Institutional Research.* San Francisco: Jossey-Bass, 1981.

Hopkins, D.S.P. "Faculty Early Retirement Programs." *Operations Research,* 1974, 22, 445–467.

Hopkins, D.S.P., and Massey, W. F. *Planning Models for Colleges and Universities.* Stanford, Calif.: Stanford University Press, 1981.

Keeney, R. L., and Raiffa, H. *Decisions with Multiple Objectives: Preferences and Value Tradeoffs.* New York: Wiley, 1976.

Kuh, G. D., and Whitt, E. J. *The Invisible Tapestry: Culture in American Colleges and Universities.* ASHE-ERIC Higher Education Research Report, no. 1. Washington, D.C.: Association for the Study of Higher Education, 1988.

McCartt, A. T. "Multiattribute Utility Models and the Tenure Process." In J. Rohrbaugh and A. T. McCartt (eds.), *Applying Decision Support Systems in Higher Education.* New Directions for Institutional Research, no. 49. San Francisco: Jossey-Bass, 1986.

McLaughlin, G. W., Montgomery, J. R., Gravely, A. R., and Mahan, B. T. "Factors in Teaching Assignments: Measuring Workload by Effort." *Research in Higher Education*, 1981, *14* (1), 3–17.

Montgomery, J. R., McLaughlin, G. W. and Mahan, B. T. "Planning and Management of Faculty Resources." Paper presented at the annual forum of the Association for Institutional Research, Minneapolis, 1981.

Peat Marwick Main & Co. *Faculty Workload at the University of Northern Iowa; Faculty Workload at the University of Iowa; Faculty Workload at Iowa State University.* New York: Peat Marwick Main & Co., 1989.

Plourde, P. J. *Experience with Analytical Models in Higher Education Management.* Amherst, Mass.: Center for Educational Management Systems, June 1976.

Ramsey, J. D., Hardwick, C. S., and Ainsworth, L. "The Academic Affairs Information System: An Aid in Resource Allocation." *Texas Tech Journal of Education*, 1981, *8* (3), 189–203.

Schroeder, R. G. "Resource Planning in University Management by Goal Programming." *Operations Research*, 1974, *22*, 700–714.

Shull, H. E. "Quantitative Assessment of Faculty Workloads." Paper presented at the annual meeting of the Association for the Study of Higher Education, Chicago, 1984.

Shulman, C. H. *Old Expectations, New Realities: The Academic Profession Revisited.* ASHE-ERIC Higher Education Research Report, no. 2. Washington, D.C.: Association for the Study of Higher Education, 1979.

Shulman, C. H. "Do Faculty Members Really Work That Hard?" *Higher Education Research Currents*, October 1980, pp. 5–12.

Spinney, D. L., and McLaughlin, G. W. "The Use of a Markov Model in Assessment of Alternate Faculty Personnel Policies." *Research in Higher Education*, 1979, *11* (3), 249–262.

Wallhaus, R. A. *A Resource Allocation and Planning Model in Higher Education.* Boulder, Colo.: National Center for Higher Education Management Systems, 1971.

Wallhaus, R. A. "Analyzing Academic Program Resource Requirements." In P. Jedamus, M. W. Peterson, and Associates (eds.), *Improving Academic Management: A Handbook of Planning and Institutional Research.* San Francisco: Jossey-Bass, 1980.

Walters, A., Mangold, J., and Haran, E.G.P. "A Comprehensive Model for Long-Range Academic Strategies." *Management Science*, 1976, *22* (7), 727–738.

Yancey, B. D. (ed.). *Applying Statistics in Institutional Research.* New Directions for Institutional Research, no. 58. San Francisco: Jossey-Bass, 1988.

Yucker, H. E. *Faculty Workload: Research, Theory, and Interpretation.* ASHE-ERIC Higher Education Research Report, no. 10. Washington, D.C.: American Association for Higher Education, 1984.

Karen D. Byers is a senior consultant in the Higher Education Management Consulting Practice at Peat Marwick Main & Company, New York.

Cynthia A. Linhart is a manager in the Higher Education Management Consulting Practice at Peat Marwick Main & Company. She served in various administrative capacities for twelve years at the University of Pittsburgh.

Michael J. Dooris is senior planning analyst in planning and analysis at The Pennsylvania State University.

The management of faculty resources requires an accurate portrait of the faculty marketplace. Available publications and data bases provide a demographic description of the faculty pipeline.

The Faculty Pipeline

Carol A. Yoannone

This chapter provides an annotated bibliography of information for colleges and universities concerned about the management of faculty resources. Resources cited include periodic reports, especially those providing demographic data; individual studies and analyses; fact books; directories; yearbooks; and educational almanacs. The bibliography also describes some major projects in progress during 1989. Though not exhaustive, it identifies important resources available to institutional researchers who wish to further analyze the topics addressed in this volume.

Individual Studies and Analyses

Bowen, H. R., and Schuster, J. H. *American Professors: A National Resource Imperiled.* New York: Oxford University Press, 1986.

Rapidly taking its position as a classic resource on faculty, this publication has been quoted in many of the sources cited in this chapter. The book, based on a national study of faculty, profiles the American professoriate. Background materials for the publication were procured through unpublished reports available from the Claremont Graduate School. These include the following:

Heveron, E. D. "Part-Time Faculty: Quantitative and Qualitative Issues in Higher Education for the 1980s."

G. G. Lozier and M. J. Dooris (eds.). *Managing Faculty Resources.*
New Directions for Institutional Research, no. 63. San Francisco: Jossey-Bass, Fall 1989.

79

Kookmees-Light, B. "The Female Professoriate."
Loyd, S. "Faculty Working Conditions and Working Environment."
Schuster, J. H. "Studying the Professoriate: Notes on Methods Used for Visiting Campuses."
Stathis-Ochoa, R. "American Professors: An Assessment of the Quality and Quantity of Faculty Performance."

Clark, S., and Corcoran, M. "The Professoriate: A Demographic Profile." *National Forum: Phi Kappa Phi Journal*, 1987, *67* (1), 28–32.
Available demographic data are used to analyze trends within the professoriate. The focus is on the distribution of faculty over institutional type; personal and social attributes of faculty members; and age and career status. Trends affecting three emergent subgroups of faculty—women, minorities, and part-time faculty—are also considered.

Drew, D. E., and Tronvig, J. A. *Assessing the Quality of National Data About Academic Scientists.* Claremont, Calif.: Claremont Graduate School, June 1988.
The authors provide a brief synopsis of various faculty surveys, including major projects conducted on a national basis, surveys done by agencies and national organizations, and a few completed on a lesser scale. The report questions the comparability of data and argues the need for consistent data to be compared over time. It contains a table comparing the items covered in six faculty surveys and reproduces the questionnaires of those studies.

Engineering Education and Practice in the United States: Foundations of Our Techno-Economic Future. Washington, D.C.: National Academy Press, 1985.
This report was prepared as part of an overall study of engineering education and practice in the United States. The study focuses on the supply of qualified doctorates, particularly with respect to the academic marketplace, and discusses the supply and demand of Ph.D.'s, women, and minorities in engineering and the engineering faculty.

Hill, M. A. *An Examination of Retirement Patterns and the Age Distribution of Faculty in Public Higher Education in New Jersey.* Revised final report to the Department of Higher Education. Trenton: New Jersey Department of Higher Education, April 22, 1988.
This report describes the recent retirement patterns of faculty members in public higher education in New Jersey. It examines and projects the age distribution of these faculty members and projects faculty retirements as well. This faculty age flow model is based on the results of two faculty surveys in New Jersey. The first survey gathered demographic informa-

tion on current faculty members, and the second on those faculty who retired during the period from 1982–83 through 1986–1987.

Hyer, P. B. "A Ten-Year Progress Report on Women Faculty at Doctorate-Granting Universities." Paper presented at the annual meeting of the American Educational Research Association, New Orleans, April 23–27, 1984. 22 pp. (ED 247 838)

Data drawn from the Higher Education General Information Survey (HEGIS) are examined to determine the status of women faculty members at doctorate-granting universities during the 1971–80 period. Preliminary and partial assessment is made of how effective federal policy has been for increasing the number of female faculty members at universities, and the extent and causes of the variation in the status of women are explored. Twenty institutions with the highest percentage of women faculty for the target years are identified.

Leslie, D. W. "Part-Time Faculty: Progress or Stagnation?" Paper presented at CUEW conference on part-time teaching in the university, York University, Toronto, May 23, 1987.

This paper discusses the dilemma postsecondary institutions are facing with part-time faculty members. Issues and trends affecting part-time faculty are examined, including the need for institutions to provide clear policy statements for part-time faculty.

Lozier, G. G., and Dooris, M. J. "Elimination of Mandatory Retirement: Anticipating Faculty Response." *Planning for Higher Education*, 1989, *17* (2).

This study utilizes data generated from two surveys of the member institutions of the Association of American Universities. Included is information on the institutions' retirement policies; a five-year summary of faculty retirements by age; and the age distribution of their full-time faculty by academic area. While the data generated from this study were not conclusive enough to affirm or deny the prospect of faculty shortages, the authors suggest that institutions should anticipate an increasing rate of faculty retirements as the 1990s progress.

Mandatory Retirement Project. Consortium on Financing Higher Education (238 Main Street, Suite 307, Cambridge, Mass. 02142).

This survey, a 1987 project sponsored by the Consortium on Financing Higher Education (COFHE), provides summary data on the basic faculty retirement plans and early-retirement plans from the COFHE membership. The report also looks at the direct and embedded costs of retirement plans. The final report is now out of print. A photocopy of the report can be obtained by contacting the COFHE.

Parks, A. W., Antonoff, S., Drake, C., Skiba, W. F., and Soberman, J. "A Survey of Programs and Services for Learning Disabled Students in Graduate and Professional Schools." *Journal of Learning Disabilities*, 1987, *20* (3), 181–185.

In an effort to obtain information about programs and services available for disabled graduate students, specifically those who are learning disabled (LD), a mail survey was sent to 703 graduate and professional schools in the United States. The return rate was 32 percent. Tables reproduce the questionnaire sent to institutions and response rates for each question. Universities with programs or support services are identified.

Pearson, W., Jr. *Black Scientists, White Society, and Colorless Science: A Study of Universalism in American Science.* Millwood, N.Y.: Associated Faculty Press, 1985.

This volume looks at the black scientist in American society, beginning with a brief historical review of blacks in the scientific community. It includes statistical tables comparing the geographical origins of American scientists by race and the quality of doctorate-granting departments producing black scientists. Consideration is given to the effects of racial status on scientific career; to the career patterns of black scientists; and to minority women scientists.

Reeves, R. A., and Galant, R. L. *An Academic Resource in Low Supply and High Demand: A Survey of Community College Recruitment Plans of General Education Faculty Over the Next Five Years.* Ann Arbor, Mich.: Washtenaw Community College, 1986. 27 pp. (ED 273 334)

Community college administrators in the nineteen-state Council of North Central Community/Junior College Region were surveyed as to how they had planned to recruit faculty in general education disciplines over the next five years. Of the 353 community and junior college administrators surveyed, 55 percent responded. Information is provided regarding anticipated positions and vacancies and planned recruitment strategies. Respondents also addressed recruitment barriers and strategies for overcoming them. The report includes a copy of the instrument sent to administrators.

Stark, J. S., Lowther, M. A., and Austin, A. "Comparative Career Accomplishments of Two Decades of Women and Men Doctoral Graduates in Education." *Research in Higher Education*, 1985, *22* (3), 219–249.

The study examines the graduate study experience and subsequent career progress of men and women doctoral graduates in the field of education. Men and women doctoral recipients from a large public university were surveyed about their study and career patterns. Tables provide statistical information comparing the patterns of graduates by gender for two time periods.

Tuckman, H. P., and Belisle, M. "New Doctorates in the Job Market: Have Opportunities Declined?" *Educational Record*, 1987, *68* (1), 32–35.

Data from the National Research Council's Survey of Doctorate Recipients (SDR), a national sample survey of doctorates in over two hundred science, engineering, and humanities fields, were used to explore recent employment trends of new doctorates. Comparisons by year are made of the number of doctorates who were employed full-time versus part-time, on postdoctoral fellowships, unemployed, or not in the labor force two years after their graduations. A table of the employment status of new doctorates by gender and year is also provided. The limits of the study are discussed.

Periodic Reports and Data Bases

"Annual Report of the Economic Status of the Profession." *Academe.*

This annual report is the definitive source of faculty salary and compensation information by institutional type, academic rank, and gender for over 2,100 four-year institutions. Appendixes provide similar data for two-year colleges and preclinical departments of medical schools.

Council of Graduate Schools/Graduate Records Examination Enrollment Survey Data, 1987. (Available from The Council of Graduate Schools in the United States, Washington, D.C.)

Preliminary results of the first annual Council of Graduate Schools/ Graduate Records Examination (CGS/GRE) enrollment survey are presented. Of the 522 institutions surveyed, 512 responded. Statistical data profiled include total graduate enrollments by institutional type and sex; institutional type and enrollment status; first-time enrollments; graduate degrees awarded by sex; and a profile of graduate enrollment by region of the country. This survey is the first of an annual data collection to produce a longitudinal data base on graduate education in the United States.

The Digest of Education Statistics, National Center for Education Statistics, Office of Educational Research and Improvement, U.S. Department of Education, Washington, D.C.

This exhaustive source of statistics on education reports data for all levels of education and is updated annually. Data have been compiled from the HEGIS report. Beginning in 1989, the Integrated Post-Secondary Education Data System (IPEDS) data will be utilized for this volume.

Engineering Education. (Published monthly by the American Society for Engineering Education.)

This journal provides an annual summary of institutional data from over 200 Canadian and U.S. colleges and universities with engineering programs. Those data include faculty size, enrollments, undergraduate and graduate degrees awarded, and other measures. The journal frequently publishes other indicators—for example, on the distribution of engineering faculty by discipline, faculty positions and vacancies (for example, faculty shortages), enrollments of special populations (women, minorities, foreign nationals), enrollment projections, and other student and faculty demographic information.

A Guide to NSF Science/Engineering Resources Data. Washington, D.C.: National Science Foundation.

The National Science Foundation (NSF) publishes detailed statistics depicting the faculty condition, and enrollment data on graduate students. The data collection activities of the NSF are numerous and include reports on the number of women and minorities in the sciences and engineering; the graduate enrollments within sciences and engineering; and the characteristics of doctoral scientists and engineers in the United States. The guide provides an overview of surveys published through the NSF, including data access and availability.

Howe, R. D., and Gilliam, M. L. *1986–87 CUPA/AASCU National Faculty Salary Survey.* Washington, D.C.: College and University Personnel Association/American Association of State Colleges and Universities, 1988.

This is an annual publication presenting faculty salary data for 261 state institutions. Faculty salaries are compared by discipline and career status.

Howe, R. D., and Gilliam, M. L. *CUPA 1986–87 National Faculty Salary Survey by Discipline and Rank in Private Colleges and Universities.* Washington, D.C.: College and University Personnel Association, 1988.

This is an annual presentation of a salary survey of 46,597 faculty members at 478 private institutions. Details include the percentage of faculty in a major area of study who hold a particular rank and comparisons of average salaries across institutions.

Mingle, J. R. *Focus on Minorities: Trends in Higher Education Participation and Success.* Denver: Education Commission of the States and the State Higher Education Executive Officers, 1987.

This report examines undergraduate and graduate enrollment rates of minorities. Demographic data related to graduate student participation include full-time enrollment in professional and graduate programs for selected years; field selection of minority Ph.D.'s in 1975 and 1985; and the number of doctorate recipients by citizenship, racial/ethnic group, and subfield.

"On Campus With Women." In *Liberal Education.* (Published four times yearly by American Association of Colleges.)

This is a quarterly newsletter of the Project on the Status and Education of Women. This publication, published within the American Association of Colleges' *Liberal Education,* covers issues and trends affecting women in higher education. Topics include academic employment and the status of women in traditionally male fields.

Splete, A. P., Austin, A. E., and Rice, R. E. *Community Commitment and Congruence: A Different Kind of Excellence.* Washington, D.C.: Council of Independent Colleges, 1987.

This is a preliminary report of a multiyear program designed to study and identify ways to improve the quality of the academic work place in liberal arts colleges. This report highlights areas affecting faculty morale and profiles ten exemplary colleges. Summary data of faculty response to a survey are provided with selected interpretations. Further reports will be issued as research is completed.

Stern, J. D., and Chandler, M. O. (eds.). *The Condition of Education.* Washington, D.C.: National Center for Education Statistics, Office of Educational Research and Improvement, U.S. Department of Education, 1988.

This annual report provides statistical information in the form of forty to fifty education indicators—key data measuring the "health" of education. The data are derived from studies carried out by the center as well as from other studies. The second of this report's two volumes contains information relevant to higher education. Trends reported include average faculty salaries by academic rank, institutional control, and type of institution. The indicators use the most recent data available, including those collected through the Higher Education General Information Survey (HEGIS). Beginning in 1989, data will be reported from the Integrated Post-Secondary Education Data System (IPEDS), an expanded version of HEGIS.

Vetter, B. M. *The Technological Marketplace: Supply and Demand for Scientists and Engineers.* Washington, D.C.: Scientific Manpower Commission, 1985.

This volume integrates most of the statistically based data available on trends in the technological employment field. Trend data over the previous decade are provided along with projections. Academic marketplace information includes tenure status of science and engineering faculty and doctorate recipients entering the work force, by field of study.

Vetter, B. M., and Babco, E. L. *Professional Women and Minorities.* Washington, D.C.: Commission on Professionals in Science and Technology, A Manpower Data Resource Service, 1986.

This comprehensive resource provides a variety of statistics in approximately four hundred charts and tables, including data on academic position by year of doctoral conferment with breakdowns by discipline. Tenure rates for minorities and women are also provided. This resource utilizes a number of sources of statistical profiles and includes a bibliography of data sources.

Compendiums

Breneman, D. W., and Youn, T.I.K. (eds.). *Academic Labor Markets and Careers.* Philadelphia: Falmer Press, 1988.

Contributors to this volume utilize methodologies from economics and sociology to analyze several dimensions of the academic "labor market." Topics include entrance into the profession; institutional mobility in academia; demographics of part-time faculty; and the academic salary differences between men and women faculty members.

Cohen, A. M., Palmer, J. C., and Zwemen, K. D. *Key Resources on Community Colleges: A Guide to the Field and Its Literature.* San Francisco: Jossey-Bass, 1986.

This guide to the community college literature summarizes over 680 books, monographs, journal articles, and research reports. Of particular note are sections concerned with locating information on staff and faculty.

The 1988 NEA Almanac of Higher Education. Washington, D.C.: National Education Association, 1988.

This publication provides an overview of American higher education. Faculty salary information is compared and detailed. General information on higher education is also presented along with a list of reference sources.

Ottinger, C. A. *Fact Book on Higher Education.* New York: American Council on Education, 1988.

This annual comprehensive information source provides tables that emphasize trends in higher education and compare data over time. Information is based on more than thirty sources. The 1988 edition provides an increased number of tables based on unpublished tabulations of government statistics available only on data tape.

Palmer, J. (ed.). *Statistical Yearbook of Community, Technical, and Junior Colleges.* Washington, D.C.: American Association of Community and Junior Colleges, 1988.

Data are presented from a survey of community, technical, and junior colleges. Faculty and professional staff data include employment by sex, professional status, full- or part-time appointment, and total numbers. Individual institutions are briefly described by state location, chief executive officer, control type, and enrollment.

Parnell, D., and Peltason, J. W. (eds.). *American Community, Technical and Junior Colleges.* New York: Macmillan, 1984.

This resource provides a comprehensive list and description of two-year postsecondary institutions. Facts about governance, academic calendar, administration, and faculty are presented.

Yearbook of Higher Education. Chicago: Marquis Professional Publications. (Published annually.)

This volume provides information on two- and four-year institutions in the United States and Canada. A composite view of each postsecondary institution is provided as well as statistics on graduate students, such as enrollment patterns and degrees awarded by field of study. Data on instructional staff include the number of full- and part-time faculty members and the average salaries of full-time faculty members. Tables providing historical and projected statistics are included.

Works in Progress

Faculty at Work. This study, being conducted by the University of Michigan's National Center for Research on Postsecondary Teaching and Learning (NCRPTL), focuses on faculty members' work activities. The faculty surveyed represent a national sample stratified by the Carnegie classification of institutions. Faculty members in English, history, political science, biology, chemistry, psychology, and sociology were asked to describe their work activities and work environments. Results of the study will be available in 1990; the questionnaire, along with the accompanying code book, can be obtained from NCRPTL.

National Academy of Sciences. Congress has appropriated money for a national study of faculty members and the effects of uncapping the mandatory retirement age on January 1, 1994. This study, originally called for in the 1986 Amendments to the Age Discrimination in Employment Act, will get underway in 1989. Contact Brett Hammond, National Academy of Sciences, Washington, D.C., for further information.

National Survey of Instructional Staff. The Center for Education Statistics of the United States Department of Education is sponsoring a survey of instructional faculty at four-year institutions. The study is being conducted by SRI International and The Pennsylvania State University's Center for the Study of Higher Education. Faculty are being surveyed on demographic data, work activities, working conditions, and their opinions on various faculty-related issues. For further information, contact James Fairweather, The Center for the Study of Higher Education, The Pennsylvania State University.

Penn State/TIAA-CREF Faculty Retirement Project. This 1989 study relies on 1987–88 data gathered from a cross-section of over one hundred participating institutions nationally. Included are institutional data (by type of college or university) on retirement policies and plans; average age at retirement (for 1981–82 through 1987–88); faculty retirements by age and discipline; and faculty distribution by age and discipline. In addition, a survey of individual faculty members provides information on factors that influence retirement planning for faculty age fifty-five and older. For further information, contact G. Gregory Lozier or Michael J. Dooris, The Pennsylvania State University.

Project on Faculty Retirement. This study is being sponsored by the American Association of University Professors, the Association of American Universities, the Consortium on Financing Higher Education, and the National Association of State Universities and Land-Grant Colleges. Data are being collected for a report analyzing the anticipated impact of the uncapping of the mandatory retirement age for professors. This project, described as a descriptive inventory, focuses on research universities and selective liberal arts colleges since the most severe repercussions from the uncapping legislation are expected in those institutional types. The study, which began in July 1988, is expected to continue at least through June 1990. For further information, contact Sharon Smith, Project on Faculty Retirement, Princeton University.

Robust Faculty Planning Model. The Consortium on Financing Higher Education is sponsoring the development of a computer model of faculty flow to retirement. The program will simulate varying situations for use in institutional planning. The model, which uses LOTUS 1-2-3, will be available at cost and is expected to be ready for distribution by the middle of 1989. For more information, contact Frederick Biedenweg at Stanford University.

White Paper on How Tenure Is Interpreted. Tenure has typically been defined by traditions, but in current times, institutions are finding the need to specify what "having tenure" entails. The Consortium on Financing Higher Education is preparing an occasional paper to analyze how tenure has been interpreted within judicial parameters and to offer general thoughts on tenure. The paper is expected to be completed by fall 1989. For further information, contact Katherine H. Hanson, Consortium on Financing Higher Education, 238 Main Street, Suite 307, Cambridge, Mass.

Carol A. Yoannone is a doctoral candidate in higher education at The Pennsylvania State University. She is currently serving as an administrative intern with the University's Division of Undergraduate Studies.

The management of academic staffing will become both more complex and more critical in the coming decade.

Responding to the Challenge

Michael J. Dooris, G. Gregory Lozier

The goal of this volume has been to explore the issues likely to impinge on the effective and efficient management of faculty at individual institutions in the decade ahead. As the preceding chapters have shown, academic managers in the 1990s will likely face a complex set of challenges in the management of faculty resources. These challenges are constantly changing and unpredictable. Nonetheless, this volume was based on the assumption that even under conditions of uncertainty, campuses can benefit by carefully preparing for and planning the management of faculty resources. In fact, we believe that planning for the prudent management of academic personnel must be part of the overall management of an institution at any time, and that in periods of change, unpredictability, and complexity, such planning becomes more—not less—critical.

Considerable evidence indicates that faculty resource management in the coming decade will be more multifaceted than in years past. In part this is because yesterday's solutions have to some extent evolved into today's problems. During the 1960s, for example, management decisions in academic personnel were driven largely by a single consideration—the need to meet burgeoning student demand. That demand was met, and institutions at the time were not overly concerned about the long-term implications for faculty demographics. Poor personnel decisions were countered by seemingly endless growth, the infusion of new resources, and the hiring of additional personnel. Although many institutions expe-

G. G. Lozier and M. J. Dooris (eds.). *Managing Faculty Resources.*
New Directions for Institutional Research, no. 63. San Francisco: Jossey-Bass, Fall 1989.

89

rienced at best stable and frequently declining real resources during the 1970s, vestiges of 1960s' human resources management have continued into the 1980s.

This approach has begun to change, however, and fairly rapidly on higher education's geologic time scale. Works such as Hopkins and Massey (1981) on human resources planning models and Baldwin and Blackburn (1983) on utilizing faculty in a period of constraint helped fill a gap in the literature in the early 1980s and were a precursor to today's growing awareness. But it was the 1986 publication of Bowen and Schuster's book on faculty as "a national resource imperiled" that dramatically crystallized attention to the interconnectedness of inadequate faculty salaries, the brain drain of Ph.D.'s to business and government, and a shrinking pool from which to draw future faculty. More recently we have seen warnings (Lozier and Dooris, 1988-89) of possible shortages as the baby boom faculty hired in the 1960s suddenly approach retirement age in the late 1990s. Such developments cut across the first five chapters of this book. These factors, along with others identified by the chapter authors, illustrate that the effective management of faculty resources is simultaneously becoming more critical and more difficult.

Each chapter in this volume has addressed the problem from a specific perspective such as affirmative action, alternative appointment types, faculty development, and so on. But some important issues, mostly relating to the national market for faculty, do not fit neatly into such categories. We offer the following for the consideration of academic managers and institutional researchers.

The Faculty Pipeline

Bowen and Schuster (1986) estimate that virtually the whole of the nation's seven hundred thousand faculty members will turn over in the next twenty-five years. This will create an unprecedented replacement demand for new professors. However, the pipeline of students preparing for careers in academe is not expanding. The number of doctorates awarded annually, which tripled during the 1960s, has remained more or less constant at about thirty-two thousand from the early 1970s through the 1980s. And the share of doctorates earned by American citizens has declined steadily; in 1987 only seven out of ten doctorates were awarded to United States citizens.

There are few signals that this situation will get better soon. The 1986 income tax reform made graduate study more burdensome financially, even as the length of time required to earn a doctorate continued to creep upward. According to the National Research Council (1989), for example, the time taken to earn a doctorate in the humanities has increased from 5.5 years in 1967 to 8.4 years in 1987. And a perception exists that faculty salaries are gradually becoming less competitive with salaries in other sectors, especially for disciplines such as mathematics and engineering—disciplines where shortages are already being felt intensely.

The dearth of students entering the pipeline is compounded not only for specific disciplines but for minority students. In particular, the number of black males earning Ph.D.'s is declining with only about three hundred degrees awarded in 1987; this is less than half the number awarded a decade earlier. During the 1980s, colleges and universities could perhaps attribute their inability to hire more minority faculty to a lack of openings for replacement hires. By contrast, over the next ten to fifteen years, open lines are likely to provide ample opportunity to increase minority representation in the professoriate—but that opportunity may go begging for want of minority students earning doctorates.

What can be done to address these daunting problems? First, faculty careers must be made more attractive, both in perception and in fact. This will require not just raising faculty salaries but getting today's faculty to identify promising students and promote the many benefits of faculty careers to them. Those benefits include intangibles such as intellectual freedom and quality-of-life considerations unique to the academy. Second, the experience of earning a doctorate can be made less onerous by improving graduate stipends, expanding opportunities for internships or fellowships, enhancing graduate housing (especially for young families), and providing affordable, high-quality day care. In addition, institutions should more carefully examine credit requirements for the baccalaureate degree. Even without the attraction of high entry salaries in such fields as engineering, the student who already took five years to earn the 135 credits for a baccalaureate degree may look less eagerly toward another three to five years of graduate school.

Institutional researchers can help by providing better information on the reasons students do or do not pursue graduate study and faculty careers. Also, researchers and planners may be able to raise administrators' awareness about problems such as the number of baccalaureate credits required for a degree, the time required to complete a doctorate, or the percentage of doctoral students who drop out without completing their degrees. They can then help to keep such topics on the management agenda.

Reward Structures

Today we see some college administrators warily moving toward the redefinition of traditional tenure policies (Mangan, 1989). This is being accompanied, not surprisingly, by a ground swell of renewed interest within faculty in merit pay and related matters (see, for example, the 1988 issue of *Academe*, devoted to this theme).

It appears that to date, experimentation with tenure policies is not a national movement. It is being carried on mostly at smaller colleges, and few of higher education's "trend-setting" institutions are involved. This may be due in part to the lessened impact these institutions expect from prospective demographic changes, including faculty shortages. Another reason for relatively little experimentation may be that such changes are generally perceived and discussed negatively as threats to tenure. It might be of greater benefit, both to faculty and to colleges and universities, to develop alternatives to traditional tenure from a positive perspective. David Leslie's chapter on creative staffing weighed the advantages and disadvantages of various appointment types. To that discussion we simply add the observation that it should be possible to develop alternatives—with regard not only to appointment types but to performance expectations—that go hand in hand with the institution of tenure. With 40 percent of current doctorate holders working outside of academe, such personnel may provide colleges and universities with a supplement to their freshly minted Ph.D.'s and could offer instructional services in some fields. Do traditional perceptions of tenure need to be altered to accommodate such appointments?

Retirement Policies

Until recently, the impending uncapping of mandatory retirement for tenured faculty led to concerns that campuses would have to cope with a surplus of elderly scholars. Those concerns led to a spate of early-retirement incentives at many institutions. However, a closer examination of faculty staffing trends and retirement patterns has led to the admission that higher education does not really know what will happen when retirements are uncapped in 1994. Researchers are becoming more concerned about the replacement of large numbers of retiring faculty than about the threat of so-called deadwood. In preparation for the uncertain future, administrators can try to enhance the attractiveness and flexibility of retirement policies, to the benefit of individuals and institutions.

At the state level, initiatives can be made to encourage faculty mobility. Two states, Georgia and Idaho, are currently considering legislation to permit portable retirement programs as alternatives to the current state-mandated system (Blumenstyk, 1989). Institutional researchers, working with their respective offices for human resources, should prepare annual reports on faculty retirements, covering age at retirement, benefits options selected, and postretirement income and activities. To capture this information, researchers will need to use a variety of methods, including analysis of institutional data bases, surveys, and exit interviews.

Challenges and Opportunities

Without concluding on an implausibly cheerful note, we do see the chance that the many challenges facing colleges and universities in the arena of faculty resources may lead to positive outcomes. The attention being paid to issues such as faculty demographics, reward structures, incentives to graduate study, and so on is overdue. So, too, may we see greater utilization of sophisticated analytical tools; policy makers may come to realize that modeling "can be extremely useful in examining an institution's options for dealing with these [mandatory retirement] changes" (Hopkins and Massey, p. 351).

Also, concerns about faculty staffing have not by and large been seen as long-term policy-making priorities on many campuses. Perhaps the current awareness will lead to such issues being more closely linked to planning and resource allocation processes. As part of that development, campuses may discover new ways of doing business, which may in turn strengthen them. For example, faculty shortages may lead to the reevaluation of narrow subdisciplinary concentrations in particular departments.

In short, it is likely that colleges and universities will to some extent be reshaped as they change their approach to faculty resources over the next ten to fifteen years. The challenge for institutional researchers in this context is not so much to predict the future but to help shape it.

References

Academe, 1988, 74 (6), entire issue.

Baldwin, R. G., and Blackburn, R. T. (eds.). *College Faculty: Versatile Human Resources in a Period of Constraint*. New Directions for Institutional Research, no. 40. San Francisco: Jossey-Bass, 1983.

Blumenstyk, G. "As 1989 Legislatures Convene, Public Colleges in Many States Face Tough Battles for Funds." *Chronicle of Higher Education*, January 4, 1989, pp. A-1, A-24–A-29.

Bowen, H. R., and Schuster, J. H. *American Professors: A National Resource Imperiled*. New York: Oxford University Press, 1986.

Hopkins, D.S.P., and Massey, W. F. *Planning Models for Colleges and Universities*. Stanford, Calif.: Stanford University Press, 1981.

Lozier, G. G., and Dooris, M. J. "Elimination of Mandatory Retirement: Anticipating Faculty Response." *Planning for Higher Education*, 1988–89, 17 (2), 1–13.

Mangan, K. S. "Colleges Are Attempting to Redefine Tenure Policies." *Chronicle of Higher Education*, March 1, 1989, pp. A-10–A-13.

National Research Council. *Summary Report 1987: Doctorate Recipients from United States Universities*. Washington, D.C.: National Research Council, 1989.

Michael J. Dooris is senior planning analyst in planning and analysis at The Pennsylvania State University.

G. Gregory Lozier is executive director of planning and analysis at The Pennsylvania State University and a member of the graduate faculty in higher education.

Index

A

Academic vice-president, and personnel policies, 6, 8

Accountability, and personnel policies, 11, 13, 15–16

Administrators, personnel policy role of, 3, 4–5, 6, 8–9, 16

Affirmative action: aspects of, 45–63; background on, 45–46; concept of, 47; conclusion on, 61–62; improving record of, 56–61; policies and procedures for, 46–49; and recruitment, 4, 5; status of, 49–51; steps in, 48; targets for, 51–57, and two-tiered profession, 38

Age Discrimination in Employment Act of 1967: 1978 amendments to, 14; 1986 amendments to, 13, 14, 22, 87

Aguirre, A., Jr., 51, 62

Ainsworth, L., 72, 77

Aisenberg, N., 5, 16

American Association of Colleges, 84–85

American Association of Community and Junior Colleges, 86

American Association of State Colleges and Universities (AASCU), 84

American Association of University Professors (AAUP), 8, 16, 28, 35, 81, 88

American Council on Education, 86

American Educational Research Association, 81

American Indian/Alaskan Native faculty, status of, 51. See also Minorities

American Society for Engineering Education, 84

Analytical techniques, for faculty resource management, 73

Andrews, H. A., 8, 10, 16

Antonoff, S., 82

Appeals, of promotion and tenure decisions, 11–12

Asian-American faculty, status of, 51. See also Minorities

Association of American Universities, 81, 88

Austin, A. E., 19, 32, 66, 67, 76, 82–83, 85

B

Babco, E. L., 47, 49, 50, 51, 63, 85–86

Baldwin, R. G., 90, 93

Becker, H. S., 23, 25, 31

Begin, J. P., 11, 16

Belisle, M., 83

Besse, R. M., 66, 76

Biedenweg, F., 88

Birnbaum, R., 66, 76

Black faculty: in pipeline, 91; and sciences, 82; status of, 50–51. See also Minorities

Blackburn, R. T., 22, 31, 69, 76, 90, 93

Bland, C., 20, 31

Bloom, A. M., 70, 76

Blumenstyk, G., 92, 93

Boston, expertise in, 39

Bowen, H. R., 19, 23, 25, 26, 31, 34, 44, 50, 62, 66, 76, 79, 90, 93

Breneman, D. W., 86

Brookes, M.C.T., 67, 76

Brown, M. K., 70, 72, 76

Burke, D. L., 3, 6, 16

Byers, K. D., 2, 65–77

C

California, University of: and affirmative action, 58; part-time faculty union at, 37

California State University, and creative staffing, 34

Campbell, W. E., 74, 76

Campus visit, recruitment policies on, 5

Canada: creative staffing in, 35, 37, 42, 81; data on, 87

D

E